# Navigating Cancer

# Navigating Cancer

Research Supported Tools to Help You Cope with
the Emotional and Physical Impact of Cancer

*Dr. Jennifer Kilkus, PhD, ABPP*

*Board Certified Clinical Health Psychologist*
*Waterford, Ireland*

WILEY

Published by John Wiley & Sons, Inc., Hoboken, New Jersey.



For general information on our other products and services or for technical support, please contact our Customer Care Department within the United States at (800) 762-2974, outside the United States at (317) 572-3993 or fax (317) 572-4002.

Wiley also publishes its books in a variety of electronic formats. Some content that appears in print may not be available in electronic formats. For more information about Wiley products, visit our web site at www.wiley.com.

***Library of Congress Cataloging-in-Publication Data has been applied for:***
Print ISBN: 9781394366927
ePDF ISBN: 9781394366941
ePUB ISBN: 9781394366934
oBook ISBN: 9781394354603

Cover Design: Wiley
Cover Image: Courtesy of Mark Hill

*This book is dedicated to all of those who have trusted me with their stories.*

*Thank you.*

*And to Rachel, who had so much more to give.*

# Contents

# Part I

# Welcome

What's in this book and how to make best use of it.

## Welcome

If you've picked up this book, that probably means that you or someone you love has been thrown into the chaos that follows a cancer diagnosis. You might feel stunned, overwhelmed, or unsure how to move forward. Please know that you are not alone in those feelings. A diagnosis of cancer is a gut-wrenching experience, and feeling completely floored by it is nearly universal.

I've witnessed the stories of thousands of people dealing with cancer in my work as clinical health psychologist. Every day, I see people face the hardest stuff of life and still find hope, joy, and meaning. So that's how I know – as impossible as it might seem right now – you *can* get to a place that feels less overwhelming.

The "how" of that, I admit, is not always straightforward. Each person's experience managing cancer is unique, and there is no "one size fits all" guide to help you to deal with it. When you're experiencing something so big and so unknown, not having a guide can be incredibly disorienting. I chose the title "Navigating Cancer" for this book because navigation is all about orienting – finding a direction and then coming up with a way to get from one place to another. Successful navigation is all about what *you* need – figuring out where you want to go and learning what routes you can take to get there. So even better than a "one size fits all," you can choose a route that is tailored to you. I hope this book can help you do that.

I found this poem from writer Sara Machnik[1] to be a moving reflection of the complicated experience of cancer:

if I could travel back in time
for just a moment
I would tell myself

you're stronger than you think
you will grieve
& find gratitude

you will make friends
& lose them
you will gain perspective
& discover purpose
you will fall into darkness
& explore a new depth of joy

It will be hard
& then it will be okay

It is a simple but powerful reflection of what cancer, and life itself, can be like: Times of fear and pain, and times of hope and meaning. Her words and experiences are unique to her, and it may not feel to you that there will ever come a point where "it will be okay." But even without things being "okay," however you define that for yourself, I absolutely believe that you can also find a way through the dark and difficult parts of this experience. You *can* get to a place where the ground feels steadier under your feet.

## How I Can Help

People have told me that a cancer diagnosis feels like a grenade has been thrown into their life. And like a grenade, there is a huge impact zone, with nearly every part of life affected. I've spent my career learning all I can to help people manage the emotional and physical fallout from cancer. I want to pass along what I've learned so that you can manage that fallout more effectively.

To start, I'll outline a model – the biopsychosocial model – that I hope can give you a better understanding of the challenges that come up during cancer and how to avoid getting stuck (or how to get "unstuck" if you're already there). Together with this model, I'll review a wide variety of research supported tools you can use to have a better quality of life.

Each chapter will include a description of different skills, examples, and exercises for practice. The skills included were deliberately chosen from a variety of different therapy models and traditions, all with solid research showing their effectiveness for people coping with cancer. Because this experience is so individual, the techniques described here are flexible and can be tailored to you. In Chapter 2, you'll have a chance to identify your habits in how you typically deal with tough things so you can find opportunities to try something new. From there, you can pick and choose the parts of the book that you might find most useful. I've included some of the most common scenarios that can come up in cancer to illustrate the techniques I outline, but I'm sure I didn't manage to cover everything. Even so, you'll find that many of the tools included can apply to other situations that aren't mentioned – even ones that aren't cancer related.

These strategies are not offered with the expectation that they can completely eliminate what you might experience because of your diagnosis or treatment. I'd *love* if that were possible. But remember the grenade. There will be an impact – you may not feel like you did before the diagnosis, even if you use every single tool without fail. So instead of thinking of these strategies as a way to make you "better" (i.e., your "precancer" self), think of them as giving you more options for coping with the challenges you're facing. The aim is to improve your quality of life and help you suffer less. Whether you are newly diagnosed, have completed treatment, or will be receiving treatment for the foreseeable future, I hope you'll find suggestions that can help things feel more manageable.

## Getting the Most Out of This Book

Learning something new is hard. Learning something new when you feel emotionally upside down is even harder. I want to outline a few things to keep in mind to help minimize frustration as you make your way through this book. Some are more emotional, while the rest are more practical. All are important to help you get as much as you can from this book.

- *Remember. It is possible to be strong and struggle at the same time.* You probably don't feel strong sometimes, or maybe ever – but being strong just means we find a way to keep going, even when it feels impossible. It also means asking for help when you need it. *Struggling* ***does not*** *mean you are failing.* You are a normal human being in an incredibly difficult situation. We all struggle. Struggling just means that you are human. Life can be really hard, and healing does not always follow a direct path. If you're criticizing yourself for struggling, try to save that energy for something more helpful.
- *Show yourself some compassion.* It is normal to be frustrated when learning something new, *especially* when your emotional and physical reserves have taken a hit from cancer treatment or recovery. Aim to be kind to yourself. Being compassionate also means paying attention to what you need. The word "cancer" shows up *a lot* in this book, and there are descriptions of people struggling with things that may overlap with your experience. If that feels overwhelming at any time, know that it's perfectly okay to take a break, or to put away this book for now.
- *You get good at what you practice.* Like with any new skill, learning these techniques takes practice. You might notice some things help right away, while others may feel more like exercising a muscle: you'll see the benefit down the road after you've built up a solid foundation of strength. You get good at what you practice – including the not-so-helpful stuff – so give yourself some time to practice something more helpful.
- *Avoid an all-or-nothing approach.* It is better to practice a skill for 15 minutes every day than to do it once or twice for an hour and then never do it again. We tend to learn better with consistent practice of a new skill.
- *Find your supporters.* If you have supportive people in your life, it may be helpful for those closest to you to know that you are trying some new things. They can help cheerlead you or they can give you some quiet space to practice if you need it. If you don't have supportive people in your life, I hope you can be that person for yourself, and keep searching for people who can be with you during tough times.
- *It's okay to need more.* If you try these strategies and find yourself still really struggling, it may be time to reach out for more support. This could be a support group, local cancer charity, individual or group

therapy, a specialist service like palliative care, or a discussion with your oncologist or primary care doctor about medication options that could help. In any case, it's important to remember that *this is perfectly okay*. It's totally normal for people struggling through cancer to need more than one type of support.

- ***You** are the person who knows best about what you need.* Not me, not your oncologist, not your well-meaning friend, or that random neighbor who thinks you should try the latest nutty cancer cure. **You** are the only one who has to live in your mind and body. **You** are the expert. So if something written in this book doesn't fit you, leave it behind. (And tell your neighbor to find a hobby).

## About the Companion Website

This book is accompanied by a companion website BCS (Ancillary):

**www.wiley.com/go/Kilkus/Navigatingcancer**

This website includes:

- Videos
- Worksheets

# Part II

## Getting an Aerial View

Building a broader understanding of what goes into health and well-being; learning your unique patterns in how you manage both emotional and physical challenges.

1

# Cancer and the Mind–Body Connection

A diagnosis of cancer can make you feel like nothing is within your control. You couldn't control your diagnosis, and there are no guarantees about what the future might look like. Even so, there may be some things you can do to help your recovery, reduce your risk of cancer recurrence, maintain remission, or improve your quality of life. This chapter is all about helping you understand how your mind, your body, and your environment all play a role in how you feel.

## The Biopsychosocial Model

Over the years, researchers have come to understand that our health is affected by our thoughts, emotions, behaviors, our relationships, and our environment. We now know that our overall health is affected by a lot more than just what's happening in the body. The "biopsychosocial model"[1] is one way to help explain how **bio**logical factors, **psycho**logical factors, and **social** factors link together to shape health and well-being. In this model, health is seen as the result of all of these different things bouncing off of each other.

This next part gets a little clinical sounding and will include some charts and images. You may be completely over medical language and science-y descriptions by now, but I *do* think it's a useful model, so I've decided to include it. It can help with organizing what can feel like a long list of challenges and clarify what's within your control and what isn't. So if you've had more than enough of medical jargon and charts and figures, feel free to skip ahead to a different point in the book.

*Navigating Cancer: Research Supported Tools to Help You Cope with the Emotional and Physical Impact of Cancer*, First Edition. Jennifer Kilkus.  Published 2026 by John Wiley & Sons, Inc.
Companion Website: www.wiley.com/go/Kilkus/Navigatingcancer

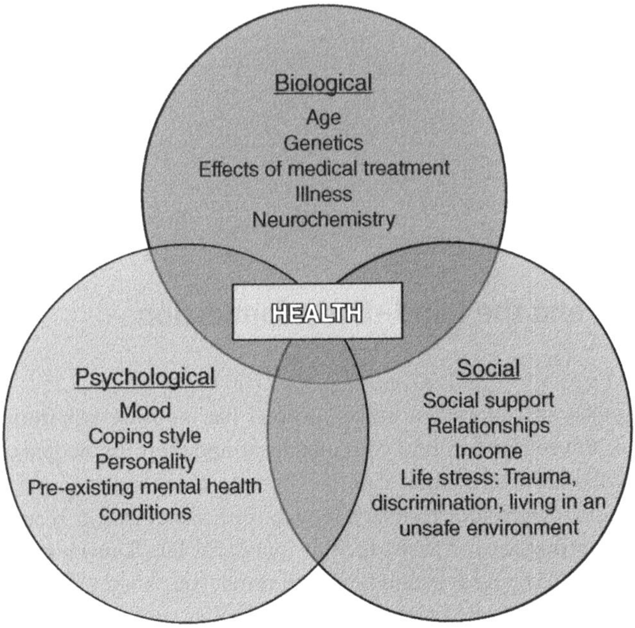


**Figure 1.1** The biopsychosocial model.

There is *a lot* going on in Figure 1.1, which is really just a reflection of the many things that can impact your health. The image describes the ways that these different elements – biological, psychological, and social/environmental – all overlap to explain your health. The **biological** circle describes things that are happening or have happened to your body that can affect your health. This could be anything from your genetics, the medicines that you take, how much good sleep you're getting, or if you have an illness you're managing. The **psychological** circle includes anything that influences how you feel emotionally: How you deal with emotions, any mental health conditions you are managing, your beliefs and predictions about yourself and the world, or your temperament. The **social** circle represents what is happening or has happened in your world: The kinds of relationships you have, financial stress, the neighborhood you live in, your family background, or history of traumatic experiences. All of these circles can overlap with and influence the others.

Let's take this model and apply it to a situation that might happen in the real world: Say you had a terrible neighbor. That would be a factor in the **social** circle. They're yelling at their family all day and night, they have a dog that never stops barking, they let their garbage pile up, and they're rude every time you try to talk to them. You notice yourself starting to be more and more on edge because of this neighbor. You have trouble relaxing and worry that you might need to move (**psychological**). Because of this, you start having trouble sleeping (**biological**), you're feeling more and more run down, and you start having heart palpitations (**biological**). You get even *more* worried (**psychological**) because you have a family history of heart disease (**biological**), and you're not sure if this stress will put you more at risk. It wouldn't take much of this before you started to feel like your health was suffering, right? So the biopsychosocial model helps us make sense of how something that may feel completely unrelated to health, like your neighbor, can actually spiral into something that makes maintaining health more challenging.

## Letting Go of Blame

What I like about this model is that it is a more accurate representation of how complex our health can be than the typical "if you just exercise and eat right you'll be healthy!" way of thinking about it. It is *really* important to try to take this on board, particularly if you have been stuck in blaming yourself for cancer. Every week, I hear from people who are torturing themselves, thinking that if only they had not smoked, eaten better, or gone to the doctor more, they would have prevented a cancer diagnosis or caught it earlier. But even nonsmoking, vegan, competitive athletes who religiously get their medical checkups get diagnosed with cancer. You'll notice that in the biopsychosocial model, there may be some things you can control, while there are other things that you can't. You obviously can't change your age, or your genetics. But you might be able to change how you manage stress, or work to improve your sleep. So while we do know there are some things that are within our control to reduce cancer risk and improve health, there are also **many** we can't. *The key is to try to find a middle ground* – accept that there are things that influence our health that we can't control, but to also remember we have the ability to change or control others.

## Understanding the Stress Response System

A big part of understanding the biopsychosocial model is understanding how health is affected by stress. You may instinctively know that it's not great for your body to be under a lot of stress, but might be wondering *how* stress actually impacts your health. Before I get into this, I want to be clear about what I'm saying about stress. While we know that chronic stress is not ideal for our bodies, there is *no definitive evidence that stress causes cancer.*[2–4] You may have heard and read otherwise. The reality is that determining causes of illness is incredibly complicated. Pointing to just one cause (stress, or trauma) oversimplifies this complex process. As of the writing of this book, research has not shown a consistent link between stress and cancer risk. Stress should be considered as one of *many* factors that influence our health, like we saw in the biopsychosocial model. Coping with stress ineffectively can lead to unhealthy behaviors that could indirectly influence cancer risk, like heavy alcohol use. The development of cancer is the result of combination of factors, some controllable and some uncontrollable, like I outlined earlier in this chapter. So why am I bringing this up?

Even if stress does not directly cause cancer, coping with stress in a healthy way can free up those resources that may be otherwise stuck in *fight*, *flight*, or *freeze* so they can be used for keeping you healthy as possible. Our bodies feel better and are less likely to freak out on the little things when we more effectively handle stress. Dealing with stress effectively gives you the best possible chance to fill your coping "well" back up, making things feel just that much easier.

## Fight, Flight, Freeze

Imagine this: you walk out your front door to start your day and you see a bear about 10 feet away. I know – unlikely (depending on where you live!) – but, if that *did* happen, you'd freak out, right? Your brain and body would *immediately* go into "DANGER" mode – a complicated series of communications in your body would get you ready to survive this situation. Stress hormones like adrenaline and cortisol would increase your heart rate and blood pressure, and slow down any process you don't need right now – like your digestion.[5–7] All of these changes work together to help you fight, run away, or "play dead." You might have heard about this before: The *fight, flight, and freeze* response. This all happens before you can even *say* the word "BEAR!"

It's an incredible system that works perfectly for emergency situations that need us to have quick reactions. It evolved for this exact scenario – for when we encounter a predator, or some other life-threatening thing, and we need our bodies to respond as quickly as possible. But sometimes our brains start to see life-threatening situations everywhere, even in situations that aren't an immediate emergency. The stress response system can get switched on over and over again like an overly sensitive car alarm that reacts the same to a leaf blowing past as it does someone trying to break-in. And because the stress response system is meant to be "in case of emergency" only, that alarm can start to wear down your body and mind. When your body and mind are worn down, the alarm gets even more sensitive, and it gets harder to switch it off.

This can happen if you're in a chronically stressful situation (like cancer), or if your brain views many situations as being stressful. Those same stress hormones that are so helpful in preparing you to survive in an emergency situation can take a toll when they repeatedly flow through your body. It can wear down your immune system, and can even create inflammation that has been linked to what researchers call "sickness behaviors" like fatigue and low mood.[8,9] So, if you're finding it hard to cope during cancer, there is a really good reason. Your body is being bombarded both by the cancer treatments, which leave you depleted, and by emotional stress, which leaves you with no reserves. You're having to draw from a nearly empty well.

## Putting It All Together

Okay – so what does all of this mean practically? Let's take a look at another example that outlines how the biopsychosocial model and the stress response system can impact how you feel.

## Keisha's Story

Reduced estrogen levels are a common challenge faced by people with breast cancer. Many of the treatments for breast cancer, as well as some other types of cancers, reduce estrogen levels or block estrogen in the body. These treatments can cause a lot of difficult symptoms – weight gain, hot flashes, sleep disruption, fatigue, and changes in mood.[10,11] These symptoms can be temporary, but they can also last for years. It's easy to imagine how these changes in the body can be overwhelming.

"Overwhelmed" is definitely a word Keisha uses to describe her experience. Keisha is a 36-year-old woman who just finished treatment for breast cancer. She is experiencing *all* of the symptoms I mentioned above and is struggling. She has been feeling more depressed and anxious lately. She's having a hard time doing the things she usually enjoys, like going to concerts, going for walks with her dog, and hanging out with her friends. She is exhausted and has been snappy at work – she even got written up at her job last week for being rude to a customer. She's having thoughts like "*I just can't stand this, I don't even recognize myself*"; "*No one will want to spend time with me when I'm like this; "I don't fit in any of my clothes, I'm uncomfortable all the time*"; "*What if I can't get it together and get fired? Then I won't be able to pay my rent and I'll be homeless!*" She is spending more time at home alone and scrolling on her phone to cope. It doesn't really make her feel better, but she feels so overwhelmed and tired she doesn't even know where to start to improve things.

Keisha is confronting a domino effect of biological, psychological, and social factors that are influencing her mental and physical health.

If we take a look at Figure 1.2, we can see how the biopsychosocial model helps explain what's going on with Keisha. There's a lot happening,

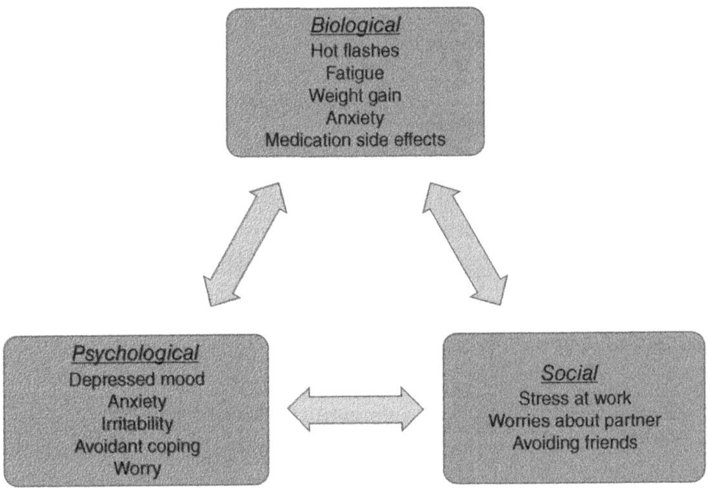


**Figure 1.2** Keisha's biopsychosocial challenges.

and each challenge seems to impact another. Let's practice with taking a look at your own model below.

**Practice Box 1.1 What does your own biopsychosocial model look like?**

**Start with what's going on biologically, with your body.** What effect has cancer or cancer treatment had on your body? How does your body feel? Do you have any challenging symptoms?

**What about psychologically?** What emotions are you feeling? What thoughts are circulating in your mind? Is there anything you do that helps you feel better?

**What social or environmental factors might be affecting you?** For example, not having enough support, or stress from other events happening in your life.

## Stuck in a Cycle

Let's go back to Keisha and look at just one of her symptoms – hot flashes – in Figure 1.3. It becomes clear pretty quickly that Keisha is stuck in an unhelpful cycle that is keeping her pretty miserable. Hot flashes often trigger anxiety for Keisha, because the symptoms mimic anxiety (feeling hot and sweaty). She's also had times where the hot flashes have been so bad, she's soaked through her clothes, and she's anxious about that happening in public. She tries to cope with anxiety by distracting herself by scrolling on her phone, which – let's be honest – is probably worsening her mood. For Keisha, this is causing some pretty negative thoughts, leading her to avoid her friends. That seems to make her feel more anxious since she isn't able to talk to them and get their support.

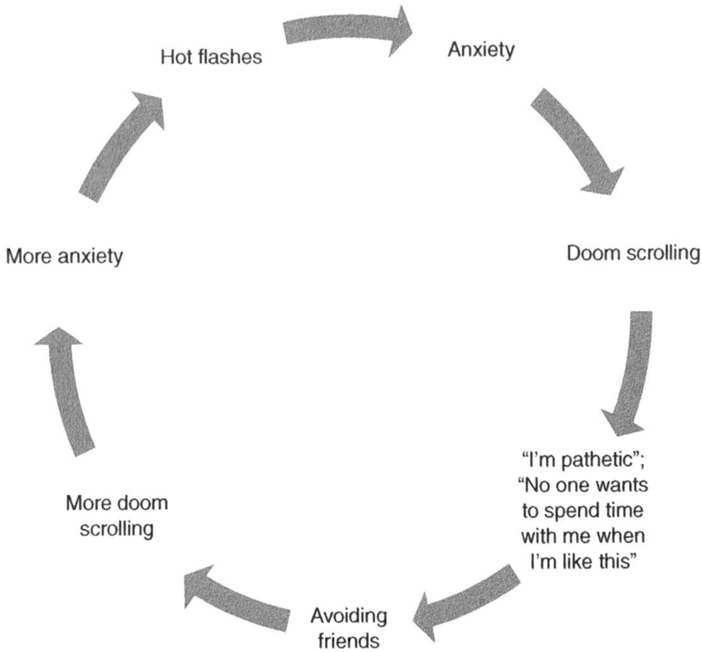


**Figure 1.3** Keisha's anxiety cycle.

She's also worried that she won't be able to find a partner who will be understanding about her cancer history. This causes more anxiety, which just seems to keep the cycle going.

While it *absolutely* makes sense that Keisha is having a hard time dealing with the many changes she is coping with postcancer, there may be some things she can try to help herself get out of this cycle. What suggestions would you make to Keisha?

| **Reflection Box 1.1 What ideas do you have for Keisha to try to get unstuck?** |
| --- |
| |

**Figure 1.4** Insomnia cycle.

Let's look at another common cycle that can happen with cancer, outlined in Figure 1.4: Sleep problems. Most people think of insomnia as being solely a medical problem, but it's actually a great example of the biopsychosocial model. The **biological** parts are usually pretty clear: Cancer can cause sleep disruption in a whole host of ways. Chemotherapy has been shown to actually change your circadian rhythm – your body's internal clock that tells you when to fall asleep and when to wake up.[12] Other biological factors, like pain or hot flashes, or the impact of medication like steroids, can also make sleep really challenging. But there is often a big **psychological** and **social**/environmental piece of sleep, too. If you've ever watched the clock and been worried about how many hours of sleep you're getting – that's psychological! Been anxious about how you're going to feel the next day? Also psychological! This can also become biological over time – the more physically wound up you become about not being able to sleep, the less likely it will be that you'll be able to. This can start causing problems pretty quickly.

Finally – what's happening **socially/environmentally** matters, too. Maybe your partner snores like a freight train, or you have a pet that loves to wake you up early. If your environment is too noisy, too hot, too cold – all of those things can make sleeping well hard.

**Practice Box 1.2 Blank cycle**

See if you can learn more about one of your own cycles by completing this blank one. Pick one of your challenges – some examples might include feeling depressed, anxious, or fatigued – and notice if there is anything happening that might be getting you stuck.

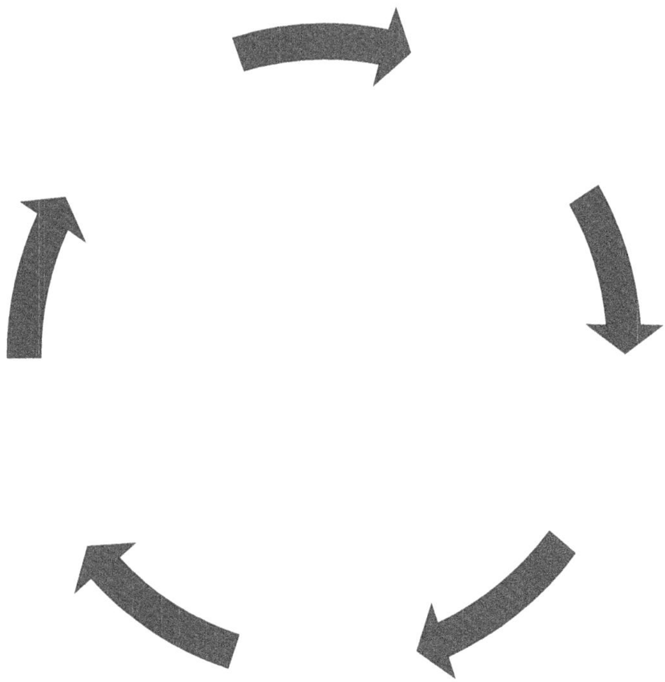

# 2

# What Does It Mean to "Cope"?

Coping with cancer is hard. It's normal to struggle to manage all of the emotional and physical challenges that come up after a diagnosis. In the last chapter, I talked about the biopsychosocial model and how there are some things you don't have any control over, while there are some you do. A big "controllable" piece of this model is how you respond to stressful situations – in other words, how you cope with the challenges facing you. This chapter describes what coping is, outlines different coping styles, and then gives you an opportunity to assess your own habits in coping so you can see where there might be healthier and more effective ways to respond to stressful situations.

## What Is Coping?

What does it actually *mean* to "cope?" Coping is what we do in response to a stressful or challenging situation so that it harms us as little as possible. Researchers[1] have developed a three-step way of thinking about this:

1. Something stressful happens.
2. We assess the situation and ourselves: *What is going on? Is the situation a threat? Is it negative? Positive? Or nothing to worry about? Do I have the tools I need to deal with it?*
3. We decide on a behavior that helps us manage the situation.

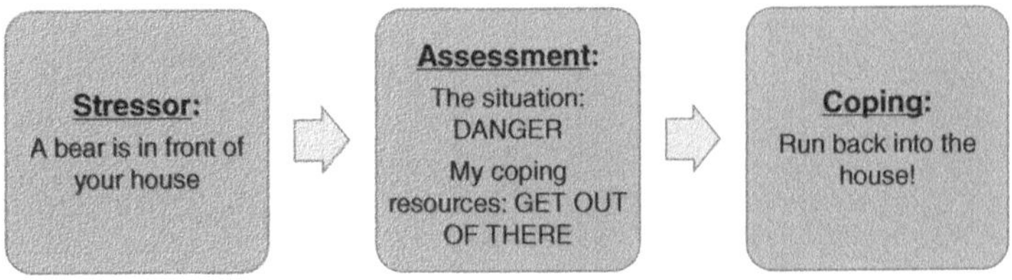


**Figure 2.1** Coping steps.

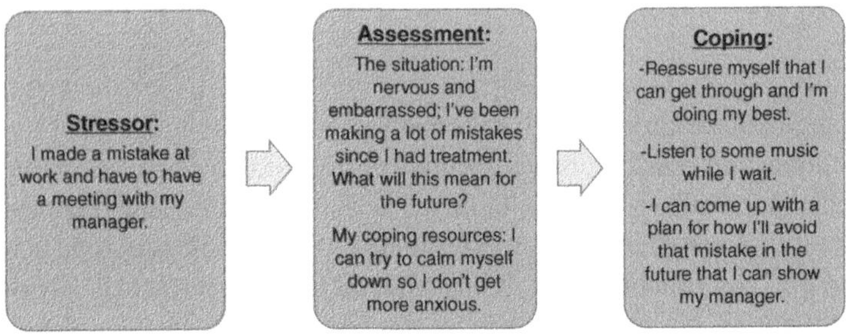


**Figure 2.2** Coping steps example.

Remember when I talked about seeing a bear in front of your house in the last chapter? Let's take a look at that again from this three-step process (Figure 2.1).

Now, this is a situation where all of this would be so scary and happen so quickly that there would be almost no way to choose a way to cope. Your body would just assess that there is danger, and get you out of there. But what about a more everyday situation?

You might notice that a lot depends on our assessment of the situation, and then the resources we have available to cope with it. And that really is the trick with managing stressful situations: How intensely we feel stress and how much it impacts our body has everything to do with how we *perceive* a stressful situation and how we *respond* to it.

Picture instead that you were in that situation and you recently had a disagreement with your manager (Figure 2.2). The assessment might go up in intensity from "I'm nervous" to a genuine fear about what will happen next, and you may even start to panic. It may be hard to remember any resources you have available to cope, and even if you do, it might be harder to use them because of how worried you are. Because of the worry, it's easy to jump to a "worst case scenario," like that you'll be fired.

Then, again, it might be even harder to cope because of how stressed you are in response. There is a lot that can happen between the stressor and then what happens next.

## Coping Styles

We all have our habits in coping, and we may not even realize what they are until things get so stressful that our ways of coping stop working, or our situation changes and we're not able to use the coping skills we usually rely on. When stress demands are higher, and our resources are lower, it becomes even harder to cope in an effective way.

Most of us aren't really taught how to cope. We usually use ways to deal with stressful situations based on what we see other people doing as we grow up. We might also experiment and find out what seems to work for us over time, but that doesn't always lead to effective long-term coping. Unfortunately, some of the habits we develop in coping may work well in the short term, but aren't that great for us in the long term.

When I was a child, my Dad had a temper. After he would get angry with us and had calmed down a little, he would take us out for ice cream. Guess who reaches out for a treat now when they're stressed? (*Me. Yes. It's me*). It's not that reaching for a treat when I'm upset is a bad thing on its own – it's not. But what if I did it every time I was upset? Or what if it was the only way I knew how to cope? Or what if instead of ice cream, it was something that might actually backfire pretty quickly, like reaching for alcohol every time I'm sad or worried?

Researchers have studied different ways of coping for decades, and they can usually be put into two different types of categories: passive and active.[2–4] Active coping strategies are ones that are considered more effective – they're better for us, and usually work better over longer periods of time. In fact, active coping has been shown to even impact our biology – when people use active coping, they have better immune function[4–7] (*There's that biopsychosocial model showing up again*)! Active coping is usually action-based and focuses on solving problems or soothing negative emotions. Examples of active coping would be going for a walk, listening to music, talking to a friend, or saying encouraging words to yourself.

Passive coping, on the other hand, tends to be less direct. This type of coping usually works by avoiding, denying, withdrawing, or numbing in response to the situation.[4] In Chapter 1, Keisha was passively coping by "doom scrolling" and avoiding her friends. Passive coping might also look like drinking alcohol or using drugs – including overusing legal or prescription drugs – or getting very busy to stay distracted. Passive coping is linked to some less-than-ideal consequences, like depression and more trouble adjusting to stressful situations.[4]

One of the (many) unfair things about a cancer diagnosis and cancer treatment is that it can make using active coping strategies much harder. So even if you are familiar with active coping strategies, you might be finding it much harder to use them because of feeling unwell. Or maybe you've had a long hospital stay, and there just isn't much to do to cope. Or maybe you're simply overwhelmed, and passive coping is the only thing that feels possible. In any case, there are a lot of reasons why you might find active coping more difficult after a diagnosis of cancer. Effective coping during cancer is all about using the right tool for the situation – assessing how you feel and what your needs are. Let's start by taking a look at how you're coping now.

## How Do I Cope?

Below (Table 2.1) you'll find a version of an assessment that has been used in research studies to look at how people cope, including people with a cancer diagnosis.[8] When answering, think about the ways you've been coping since your diagnosis. If you're dealing with something that's happened recently, like if you have an upcoming surgery, or if you've recently gotten some gut-wrenching news, you might find it more helpful to answer in response to how you've been coping about that particular situation rather than cancer in general.

These questions ask what you have been doing to cope with this situation. We're trying to find out how often or how much you've been doing what each question asks, so it doesn't matter if it is working or not. Right now, we're just looking to find out whether or not you're doing it. This is just for you, so don't worry about whether it's the "right" or "wrong" way to cope. Use the following scale to choose a number for each question:

**1** = I haven't been doing this at all.
**2** = I've been doing this a little bit.
**3** = I've been doing this a medium amount.
**4** = I've been doing this a lot.

**Table 2.1** Coping styles assessment.

| | Rating (1–4) How often? | Rating (1–4) How helpful? |
|---|---|---|
| 1. I've been turning to work to take my mind off things. | | |
| 2. I've been concentrating my efforts on doing something about the situation I'm in. | | |
| 3. I've been saying to myself "this isn't real." | | |
| 4. I've been using alcohol or other drugs to make myself feel better. | | |
| 5. I've been getting emotional support from others. | | |
| 6. I've been giving up trying to deal with it. | | |
| 7. I've been taking action to try to make the situation better. | | |
| 8. I've been refusing to believe that it has happened. | | |
| 9. I've been saying things to let my unpleasant feelings escape. | | |
| 10. I've been getting help and advice from people. | | |
| 11. I've been using alcohol or drugs to help me get through it. | | |
| 12. I've been trying to see it in a different light, to make it seem more positive. | | |
| 13. I've been criticizing myself. | | |
| 14. I've been trying to come up with a strategy about what to do. | | |
| 15. I've been getting comfort and understanding from someone. | | |
| 16. I've been giving up the attempt to cope. | | |
| 17. I've been looking for something good in what's happening. | | |
| 18. I've been making jokes about it. | | |

*(Continued)*

**Table 2.1** (Continued)

| | Rating (1–4) How often? | Rating (1–4) How helpful? |
|---|---|---|
| 19. I've been doing something to think about it less, like going to movies, watching TV, reading, daydreaming, sleeping, or shopping. | | |
| 20. I've been accepting the reality of the fact that it happened. | | |
| 21. I've been expressing my negative feelings. | | |
| 22. I've been trying to find comfort in my religion or spiritual beliefs. | | |
| 23. I've been trying to get advice or help from other people about what to do. | | |
| 24. I've been learning to live with it. | | |
| 25. I've been thinking about what steps to take. | | |
| 26. I've been blaming myself for things that happened. | | |
| 27. I've been praying or meditating. | | |
| 28. I've been making fun of the situation. | | |

Now, take a look at your ratings. You might find some patterns. The more "3" and "4" answers you have, the more often you are relying on that particular type of coping. If you use the scale key below, you can get even more specific about any patterns. Some of those patterns may lean toward more active (for example, questions 2, 5, and 7), while others may be more reflective of a passive way of coping (questions 3, 4, and 16). You might find that you're not doing much coping at all. No "right" or "wrong" here – this is all just information for you to use to assess what's happening with coping right now.

## Coping Questionnaire Scale Key

Self-distraction: Items 1 and 19
Active coping: Items 2 and 7

Denial: Items 3 and 8
Substance use: Items 4 and 11
Getting emotional support: Items 5 and 15
Getting advice: Items 10 and 23
Withdrawing: Items 6 and 16
Venting: Items 9 and 21
Positive reframing: Items 12 and 17
Planning: Items 14 and 25
Humor: Items 18 and 28
Acceptance: Items 20 and 24
Religion: Items 22 and 27
Self-blame: Items 13 and 26

## Doing What Works

Earlier in this chapter, I mentioned that researchers agree that active coping is generally more helpful than passive coping. While that might usually be true, I've found that for people going through cancer, it's not so straightforward. What is effective for coping during cancer really depends on what works for you, in each particular situation, with the amount of energy you have available to you. For example – problem solving is generally considered a helpful active coping strategy. But what if (like is often the case with cancer), the problem can't be solved? In that case, using problem solving to cope may just lead to worry and overthinking. Another example is distraction. Distracting yourself is usually considered a more passive way of coping. But again, sometimes with cancer, the reality may be different. When you're really feeling unwell, or right before a procedure or scan, you may just need to distract as much as you possibly can just to get through it. The goal is to pay attention to *what* works for you and *when*, so you can find the most helpful way to cope in each situation.

Early in my career, I had to have a scary medical procedure done. Nothing life threatening, but pretty uncomfortable and vulnerable. I thought to myself, "*I'm a psychologist! I teach coping skills for a living! To people who have to do this kind of stuff all the time. I've got this!* " (**Spoiler alert**: *I did not have this*). I was totally overconfident and completely unprepared for how physically anxious I became. I just couldn't calm myself, even with my "expert knowledge," and the doctor had to keep taking breaks because I was so overwhelmed. I ended up being really tearful and unsettled the entire rest of the day. And if I'm being honest, I also ended up feeling a little bit like a failure and a fraud.

I learned a few really important lessons that day. I learned that my "expert knowledge" did not in any way protect me from being like any other human in an unfamiliar and frightening medical situation (...*Obviously*). I also completely overestimated my ability to cope in the moment, and because of that, I was unprepared. That expert knowledge would have been useful, if only I had been prepared to apply it. I'm not sure if I expected it to act as some mystical forcefield, or what – a humbling experience, but one that was so important for me to have.

Unfortunately, I had to repeat this procedure a few months later. This time, though, I was ready. I found the loudest, screamiest, most empowering music I could find and made sure I had it loaded on my phone and ready to go. I arrived in the clinic room with headphones in hand and let my doctor know I was going to be mentally unavailable during the procedure, and if he needed me for anything to just tap me on the shoulder. 100% more effective.

Let's take another look at those questions again, this time with an eye for how helpful your most commonly used strategies are. This time, instead of answering about how often you use these ways of coping, I'd like you to ask yourself how helpful they are. We'll use the same 1–4 scale, but assessing helpfulness this time:

**1** = Not helpful at all
**2** = Sometimes helpful, but not for long
**3** = Helpful more often than not
**4** = Helpful almost all the time

What did you notice this time? Are the ways you are coping most often actually the most helpful?

Below you'll find some more questions to reflect on what you've learned about coping styles.

| **Reflection Box 2.1 How has coping changed during cancer?** |
| --- |
| How has your coping changed during cancer? |

Are there ways of coping that you relied on before cancer that you'd like to do more of?

What are the barriers to you coping the way that's most helpful?

Are there some situations that you think certain types of coping would be more effective than others?

## Some Coping "Rules of Thumb"

Trying to figure out the most effective ways to cope during cancer can be confusing. How you're feeling, both physically and emotionally, can be a "moving target," with a lot of ups and downs. Here are a handful of tips to keep in mind as you keep navigating the healthiest ways for you to approach the challenging situations that come up during cancer.

- Sometimes, coping is about keeping things from getting worse, instead of feeling better right away. Cancer is incredibly difficult, and coping well some days may be as simple as getting yourself out of bed. Celebrate the small wins – they count too.
- A quick guide to helping yourself cope is evaluating: *is the situation controllable or uncontrollable*? If the situation is *controllable* – it may be most helpful to take action by problem solving. If it's *uncontrollable* – focus on soothing whatever emotions you're feeling. Listen to music, talk to a friend, watch something funny – the aim is simply to help yourself get through it. Avoid wasting your energy trying to "fix" an uncontrollable situation.
- It's usually best to rely on a variety of types of coping strategies rather than just one. That way, if the situation doesn't allow for your "go to," you'll have a back-up plan. If you tend to rely on just one method of coping, see if you can push yourself a bit to try a different one and see how that feels.

- There is no "right" way to cope. But (and absolutely no judgments here!), relying on alcohol, nicotine, or other drugs is not the most effective for coping in the long term. They can also interfere with your treatment or increase your risk of a recurrence, so if you're finding it hard to cut back, talk to your doctor to see what ideas they have to help.

# Part III

# Laying the Groundwork

Understanding how self-compassion, mindfulness, and acceptance can give you a solid foundation for dealing with things outside of your control.

3

# Making Friends with Yourself

If this chapter title is making you worry that we've taken a sharp left turn into some "touchy feely" territory – you're absolutely right. (*Sorry!*). This chapter is all about developing kindness toward yourself.

Why is this important? After years of working with people with cancer, I continue to be amazed at how hard people are on themselves while dealing with it. I always expected that this would be the *one time* that people felt like they could give themselves a break. Look at the situation – you've been diagnosed with a serious illness, with few guarantees about what might happen with it in the future. Your entire life is disrupted and there is no clear end date – there may not even be an end date. You may have to have treatments that are incredibly harsh and that can have long-lasting effects. Wouldn't that warrant a little bit of compassion for yourself? Turns out – that's often not that case. Why is that?

Consider the narratives that usually surround cancer. The language used describes people with cancer as "fighters" and "warriors," who are "triumphing" over cancer. It doesn't allow any space for struggle. It also opens up the door for unreasonable blame, implying that if someone dies from cancer, they "lost." That blame is misdirected: The *treatment* failed, *not* the person with cancer. But it can be hard not to take on that story because it's so widespread.

This way of describing the experience of cancer reflects wider cultural narratives all over the world about how to manage challenges. We are taught that when things are hard, we just need to "suck it up" and keep going. But what happens if you are finding it hard to do that? Because the hard thing is just SO hard, or because it just keeps going on and on? Instead

*Navigating Cancer: Research Supported Tools to Help You Cope with the Emotional and Physical Impact of Cancer*, First Edition. Jennifer Kilkus.  Published 2026 by John Wiley & Sons, Inc.
Companion Website: www.wiley.com/go/Kilkus/Navigatingcancer

of viewing those narratives as the problem, we tend to label *ourselves* as the problem, leading to *more* suffering on top of an already terrible situation.

I'm including this chapter near the beginning for a reason – nearly every other situation that we'll cover in this book will require you to find a bit of kindness toward yourself. I truly believe – and research supports me on this – *being harsh toward ourselves has no value.*[1–3] If you're worried that being kind to yourself means that you'll be unmotivated, it will make you weak, that it's self-indulgent, that it's just feeling sorry for yourself, that you're being selfish – let me reassure you. *Developing kindness toward yourself simply means that you treat yourself the same way that you would someone else you care about.* That's it! No need to tie yourself up in knots.

## The Three Components of Self-compassion

Kristen Neff is a psychologist and researcher that has been studying self-compassion for more than 20 years. Her work has laid the foundation for challenging some of the myths around self-compassion. She outlines three main building blocks of self-compassion: Self-kindness, common humanity, and mindfulness.[4] I'll talk about each of these elements and ask you to reflect along the way to see where there may be opportunities to connect to your inner coach.

### Self-kindness

Self-kindness is all about getting away from self-criticism, judgment, and beating yourself up. Imagine you're struggling with the impact of treatment. If you tend to be hard on yourself, you might think something like, "*I can't do ANYTHING. I should be better by now! I'm worthless!*" Pretty harsh, right? Of course, it's understandable to be frustrated about the impact of treatment. But a self-kindness approach would focus more on being supportive, encouraging, and accepting. Think of it like this – have you ever had a really good coach or teacher? If so, my guess is that they were encouraging, motivating, and kind. They didn't make you feel terrible about yourself – instead, they noticed your strengths, and were kind about improving weaker areas. No need to be a drill sergeant with yourself – aim for an encouraging coach. That might sound more like, "*These treatments are HORRIBLE and really making life harder. It's really frustrating because I can't do everything I usually do, but I guess I have to take things day by day.*" See the difference? You're not feeling sorry for yourself. You're simply understanding the context and avoiding getting stuck in unproductive thinking – while also validating the reality of what's happening.

It may be hard to start thinking about this in a different way. Many of us were taught that a harsh approach is the best way to motivate ourselves, or to keep ourselves from being "weak." More often than not, though, we will talk to ourselves in ways that we would never speak to people we care about. Try these exercises below, and start taking note of your self-critical voice. Is it actually effective in helping you manage challenges?

**Reflection Box 3.1 How do you talk to yourself?**

How do you talk to yourself when you make a mistake, or when you're struggling? What words do you use?

What tone of voice do you use – for example, are you patient? Harsh? Angry?

Is the voice yours? If not, whose is it? Could it be someone you've known in the past who has been critical of you?

**Practice Box 3.1 Self-kindness**

Now experiment with self-kindness. Imagine a recent situation where you've struggled, or you've felt down on yourself. What would you say to someone you cared about? Aim for being understanding, but also constructive.

## Common Humanity

The idea of common humanity is for us to remember that we are human beings. And like *every single other* human being, we struggle, we make mistakes, and don't get it right 100% of the time. For whatever reason, it seems difficult for us to actually remember this. We can wind up feeling like we're the only ones suffering, that everyone else has it all figured out, and we're the only ones in pain. That somehow, we've done something wrong if we're suffering.

Let's consider again the example above of feeling frustrated with recovering from treatment. Approaching this with common humanity would sound something like this: "*I'm not worthless for struggling with this treatment. Everyone has a hard time – it's cancer treatment, after all! Expecting myself to sail through it is pretty unfair.*" When we can stop expecting perfection from ourselves and remember that we're not alone, things can feel much more manageable.

**Reflection Box 3.2 We all struggle**

Being human means that we struggle. We're not alone in this – **all** humans struggle. Think of a time when you thought you were "the only one," only to find out that someone else experienced that, too. Maybe it was an embarrassing situation or a painful experience that you learned someone else had shared.

Take a moment to reflect on the emotions you felt when you were alone in that experience. Make some notes below.

Now, reflect on what emotions came up when you learned someone else had shared that experience.

**Practice Box 3.2 Common humanity**

Let's try practicing connecting to common humanity. Go back to that same difficult experience you thought about earlier when you were practicing self-kindness. Now, try to *validate* your experience – that it's perfectly normal to feel the way you are feeling, and that you are not alone in those feelings. Most people on the planet have probably had similar feelings. It may be a simple phrase, such as *"I'm not alone,"* or it may help to get more specific: *"I remember that person in the support group saying they felt the same way. This might be more common than I realized."*

## Mindfulness

The third component of self-compassion is mindfulness. Mindfulness is a complex topic that could take up an entire book on its own. We'll be coming back to it and its different applications later on. For now, we'll stick to the basics: Being mindful of your emotional experience means being able to be aware of it without *hanging onto it*, or *pushing it away*. Let's think back to that assessment of how you cope. You may have noticed a tendency to ruminate – to turn something over and over in your mind, rehearsing situations or conversations, revisiting images of something negative that's happened in the past, or worrying about the "what ifs" of the future. That's "hanging on." Or you may have noticed the opposite – a habit of pushing painful emotions or thoughts away, avoiding or numbing them, or distracting yourself. You may be somewhere in the middle, and use a little of both. We *all* do this to some degree.

The problem is that when we get tangled up with our thoughts or feelings or try to escape them, we don't really have the opportunity to practice being more self-compassionate. Instead, we may get so caught up in these patterns that they just keep churning on without change. It can be hard to even be aware of how we respond in difficult moments because these patterns can be so automatic. You may have noticed that earlier in the chapter if you tried the reflection and practice exercises. It's hard to make a change when we're not aware of how we're actually reacting in the present.

Let's go back to that example of frustration with the slow pace of recovering from treatment, again. Rather than getting caught up in the commentary of the mind, a mindful approach would just be to observe and describe what's happening in real-time. "*I'm feeling my muscles tense and my fists clench. I'm breathing faster and my cheeks are hot. My chest feels tight. I'm noticing myself wishing this wasn't happening and feeling a little tearful. I feel sad, and angry, too. I'm having to work really hard to not criticize myself.*"

Okay, so now what? Now that you're *aware* of how you're feeling, you can do something productive in response, instead of getting caught going down a rabbit hole of thoughts or trying to get away from what you're feeling. There may be an opportunity to see where there is a choice to take care of what you need in the moment. The person in this scenario is pretty physically distressed. Maybe they could use some cold water on their face, or to try to slow down their breathing. They're also feeling a few different emotions and feeling a pull toward being self-critical – maybe they need to find that bit of self-kindness or common humanity to reassure themselves. Whatever is needed, mindfulness gives you a "pause button" to check in with yourself before ricocheting off into wherever your thoughts and emotions want to take you.

**Practice Box 3.3 Reflection on a difficult experience**

Let's go back to that same difficult experience you identified one more time. See if you can describe your response to the situation as if you're observing from the outside.

How does your body feel – any areas of tension or discomfort? Where?

How about emotions – what do you think you were feeling during this situation? Try to let yourself be with these difficult feelings without escaping or minimizing them, or getting too caught up in what stories your mind may want to tell you.

What was going through your mind at the time?

## Finding Your Self-compassionate Voice

Now that you know a little more about what goes into self-compassion, we can start to build a connection to a friendlier internal dialogue. Everyone needs something a little different, so it may take some experimentation. Because our thought patterns can be so automatic, it can take time to start to change them. It can be useful to come up with some helpful, kind phrases ahead of time. That way, you can be prepared the next time you need to hear from your kind and motivating coach.

You can even keep them on a sticky note on the bathroom mirror, in your notes app on your phone, or on the fridge – anywhere you may see them often and can rehearse them. I personally like keeping them with me. That way, if you are in a situation where you are not at home and you need some encouragement, you can pull out the list then and there.

Some examples might be:

- This is really hard, but I can get through it.
- I'm okay.
- I am not alone, other people struggle too.
- I'm doing the best I can.
- I can have a hard time and still be strong.
- Recovering takes time.
- I'm not a superhero.

This can be anything that you would find encouraging and helpful in the moment. It could be a song lyric, a prayer, a quote, or anything that you have used in the past that has helped you get through tough times. The important part is that it is tailored to you and is telling you something you really need to hear. Again, if you're finding it difficult to come up with something, try to picture what you might say to someone you really care about when they are having a hard time.

| **Practice Box 3.4 Encouraging words** |
| --- |
| See if you can find some of your own encouraging words here. |

# 4

# Building Awareness and Learning to Let Go

In the last chapter, I mentioned how automatic our responses can be when we're upset. You may not have even been aware that you had particular patterns in how you react to stress, or how you cope. Often, our patterns can become so ingrained – so automatic – that they can be challenging to change. But we can develop what I think is a superpower – an awareness of our patterns that allows us to make changes to cope more effectively.

Have you ever found yourself absentmindedly putting milk in the cupboard instead of the fridge? Or looking for your phone while it's in your hand? That's you on autopilot. And we're on autopilot *a lot*. Busy lives and a million ways to be distracted leaves a lot of opportunity to be somewhere in our minds that's far away from what's actually happening right now. That's not *always* a bad thing. For instance, you've probably heard of people having a great idea come to them in the shower. Sometimes, mind wandering allows for us to make connections we wouldn't make if we were thinking through things analytically every moment. But other times being on autopilot takes us further away from important emotional or physical signals. Those emotional and physical signals are communications that tell us what we need and give us insight into potentially unhelpful coping patterns. Building awareness of these communications provides an essential foundation for taking good care of yourself both physically and emotionally. In this chapter, we'll take a look at the practice of mindfulness as a way to develop awareness, get into the tricky subject of acceptance, and start to think through what it looks like to "let go."

*Navigating Cancer: Research Supported Tools to Help You Cope with the Emotional and Physical Impact of Cancer*, First Edition. Jennifer Kilkus.  Published 2026 by John Wiley & Sons, Inc.
Companion Website: www.wiley.com/go/Kilkus/Navigatingcancer

## What Does It Mean to Be Mindful?

When I bring up mindfulness in therapy sessions, I often get met with a sigh and "yeah, I've tried that – it doesn't work for me." Sometimes accompanied by an eye roll. And I *totally* get it. Mindfulness has become a huge buzz word, and it's being sold as the solution to everything from anxiety to increasing work productivity. And that's a shame, because all of this buzz seems to have confused what mindfulness is and how it can be helpful for coping with challenging situations. There seems to be a message being sold that if you just practice mindfulness, then somehow you'll be totally relaxed and unruffled all the time (which, I'm sorry to tell you, is impossible for 99% of us). Mindfulness also gets confused as being the same as meditation, when really, there is a lot more that falls under the umbrella of mindfulness than you might think.

Mindfulness has long, long history, originating in the Buddhist tradition of *sati* (attention/memory).[1] In the Western world, the practice has been studied in psychology and psychiatry since the 1970s for how it can help people manage emotions. But what is it, exactly? At its core, mindfulness is the practice of paying attention – so, the opposite of autopilot. But it's not just paying attention. It's *how* we pay attention. Mindfulness is about paying attention to what's happening *here and now*, and doing that in a way that is on purpose and nonjudgmental.[2]

Think about where your mind usually is when you're upset. It's probably not on the present, right? Most likely, you're either focused on the future – the "what if" or "worst case" – or you're focused on the past – getting stuck on things you can't change or control. There probably isn't much happening that is purposeful, either. Instead, you might feel like you've been hijacked by your mind, and it's driving the car instead of you. And nonjudgmental? No way! We're constantly judging when we're upset! **Ourselves** – "I shouldn't feel this way," "I shouldn't have done that," "What's wrong with me?!"; **Others** – "Why can't they just show up for me?," "They should know what I need," "What an idiot!"; And **our experience** – "Why did this have to happen to me?," "I can't stand this!." A lot of fuel to fan the flames of our already tough experiences. Mindfulness practice is one way to start to turn down the temperature by just focusing just on what *is*, instead of the chaos our minds can create. Instead of getting stuck in all that criticism, judgment, and how we think things *should* be, we instead try to shift to *accepting* things as they are, right now, to allow tough emotional and physical experiences to pass.

## The A Word

Okay – I've brought up the A Word. Acceptance. This is another word, like mindfulness, that gets interesting facial expressions when I bring it up. And no wonder, right? Acceptance during cancer is usually brought up in a way that is pretty invalidating. "You just have to accept it"; "It is what it is!," or an accusation of, "You're not accepting this, you need to move on!." *Yikes.* This way of talking about acceptance, at best, minimizes how difficult it can be to navigate a really challenging circumstance. At worst, it can communicate that you need to shut down your feelings and be passive about your situation. It doesn't provide any guidance around what it looks like to "accept," or how to go from struggling to acceptance.

So I want to be clear about what I mean when I talk about acceptance. Acceptance, the way I see it, doesn't require having to be okay with something *at all*. It also isn't passive. You can accept your circumstances and still be pissed off, or sad. You can also still try to change the situation if you need to. Acceptance really just means that you're not fighting yourself about the tough situation you have in front of you.

In my study of mindfulness, I came across the following equation that I think illustrates this point really well[2]:

$$\textbf{\textit{Suffering}} = \textbf{\textit{Pain}} \times \textbf{\textit{Resistance}}$$

The idea here is that we *all* experience pain simply because we are human and living our lives can be painful. Our human selves have the capacity to feel intense emotional pain and excruciating physical pain. The amount we *suffer* in response to pain, however, depends on how much resistance we bring to that pain. All of that "not wanting" and "should/should not-ing" we do in our minds is *multiplying* the amount of pain we feel. This can happen physically, too; when we're in physical pain, we can often add resistance by clenching, tightening, or bracing against the pain, which, unfortunately, can often actually make pain signals even more intense. So not only are we in pain, but now that pain is intensified by all that we're adding to it. **We suffer more when we get stuck in wanting things to be different than how they actually are.**

Please don't mistake me: I am not at all minimizing any of the genuine pain that can come alongside cancer and cancer treatment. I'm suggesting that you keep an eye out for any pain that you may unintentionally be adding by struggling with yourself or your situation. There is nothing and no one to blame here – this is part of what we all do as humans confronting a painful experience. My only aim is to encourage you to notice any patterns in your mind and body that might intensify what you are feeling.

I also want to make it clear that acceptance is a process. You can't push yourself into it and neither can anyone else. Everyone has their own timeline, and sometimes, you need to wrestle with anger or denial before you get to a place that feels more accepting.

**Reflection Box 4.1 Struggling with acceptance**

Can you think any times when you were having trouble accepting things as they were?

Were there ways that you were resisting the situation? It could show up in thoughts like "It shouldn't be this way." Or behaviors like avoiding dealing with the situation – for example, not taking a medication that you know will help you feel better because you don't want to have to take so many pills.

Was there any physical resistance, like clenching your jaw, or tensing your body in anticipation of pain?

## Learning to Let Go

So far, we've covered what it means to be mindful and the challenges in accepting things as they are. The more thinking we do, particularly of the unhelpful variety, the harder it is to just "be" with things as they are. We can be distracted or on autopilot, where we're just not paying attention to what we're feeling. We might also be escaping or avoiding painful experiences, by getting really busy or pushing away thoughts and feelings to focus on other things. We can also resist reality by getting tangled up in unhelpful mental chatter. Starting to "let go" means being able to get out of our heads and into what we're experiencing in the here and now.

There have been *a lot* of articles and books written on how to practice mindfulness, so it can be confusing to start. It might be helpful to think of mindfulness practice in two different ways: Informal practice and formal practice.[3] **Informal** mindfulness practice is usually neglected when people talk about mindfulness. Informal practice just means trying to apply your full attention at any time, while doing anything you normally do during the day. It is an intentional shift from autopilot with the goal of developing more awareness of your experience. You can try this with anything you do during the day that is normally an opportunity for your mind to wander, such as brushing your teeth, doing the dishes, or eating a meal. Your only task is to just notice all that you can about what you are doing – the sounds, smells, and sights of the experience – and when you become aware that your mind has wandered off, you (kindly!) try to redirect your attention back to experiencing.

This type of practice is great because you don't have to sit and meditate. You can bring your attention to anything you're doing – including exercise – and that is a form of mindfulness practice. The idea is simply to build awareness of yourself and your experience by paying attention to what's happening in the present. Over time, you get better at redirecting your attention from wherever your mind wanders back to your experience in the here and now. Obviously, there is nothing magical or mystical about washing dishes or brushing your teeth. But it does allow you to get better practiced at noticing how you feel, where your mind goes, and then bringing yourself back to the present. You'll find that paying attention to *now* allows you an opportunity to observe your thought patterns, and those emotional and physical signals I mentioned early in the chapter that can get lost in autopilot.

**Formal** mindfulness practice is what most people think of when they hear the word mindfulness. Formal practice involves setting aside a particular period of time to intentionally meditate. Formal practice builds a discipline of practice that builds up the skill of present-moment awareness over time, so that when you need it, it's there. Again, this may not be your thing, and it doesn't have to be. It is just another option for trying to develop a practice of noticing yourself and practicing paying attention, so that you can start to let go of unhelpful patterns.

So where does the "letting go" part come in? Once you start to get more familiar with your emotional and physical patterns, you have an opportunity to make a decision about what to do next. You can start to ask yourself questions like; Is it helpful for me to stay here in my mind? Is there something here that needs to be felt, or something that this is teaching me? Am I possibly fueling an emotional fire? Is there something my body needs that is trying to get my attention? *Then* if you think that it's time to "change the channel," you can shift your attention to something in the present that may be a more helpful place for your mind to be.

## Getting Started

If you're new to mindfulness practice, there's a great step-by-step outlined in Dialectical Behavior Therapy[4] that can help with how to get started:

### The "What" to Do

1. **Observe:**
   Pay attention to whatever you notice. This may be thoughts, sounds, emotions, or body sensations. Try to observe without reacting. Notice a tendency to judge or to try to change what you're noticing. Try to stay in the present moment without pushing away or clinging to any thoughts, feelings, or experiences. It can be useful to choose an anchor as a way to focus your attention in the present. An "anchor" is something you can use to redirect your attention back to when you notice your mind wandering. This can be your breath, it can be sounds, it can be a physical sensation like warm water on your skin – it doesn't matter what it is, as long as it's something you can observe in the present. Experiment with this and see what type of "anchor" may hold your attention best.
2. **Describe:**
   Put words to your experience. When a thought, emotion, or physical sensation comes up, you can label it – "worrying," "thinking," "planning"; or describe it – "My chest is tight," "I feel pain in my

leg." Try not to get caught up in the content, or the "why" – instead, try to stick with the "what."

3. **Participate:**
   Try to fully *be* in each moment – stay in the "here and now." Whenever your mind has wandered to unhelpful thoughts or painful emotions, observe them, describe them, and then bring your attention back to your anchor. Try to imagine your thoughts or emotions being like clouds in the sky, or like leaves floating by on a stream. You can notice them, watch them drift off without trying to change them, and then bring your attention back to your "here and now" anchor.

### The "How" to Do It

In mindfulness meditation practice, the "how" can be just as important as the "what." Think about this as the attitude you're bringing to the practice. Try to set aside any expectations for what you *should* feel, and just try to be with what you notice. If you're bored, that's something to notice. If you're frustrated, just notice that, too. If you're relaxed – fantastic, but that's actually not the point. The point is just to notice. With that noticing, you'll build up a solid foundation of awareness in the day-to-day so when you are feeling stressed or overwhelmed, you can catch yourself wandering to unhelpful places. Then, you can start to build the skill of redirecting your attention to somewhere that feels more helpful. Think of your mind like an untrained puppy – it's busy, it's energetic, and it can get into the garbage and chew up your favorite shoes. Instead of being angry at the puppy, try to gently and patiently continue to train it until it gets into less trouble over time.

## Things to Note

- It's normal to feel a bit worse at first. If you've been used to pushing your thoughts and feelings away, you might notice yourself feeling more upset when you give yourself space to pay attention to what's going on for you. A lot of us have the habit of staying so busy that our thoughts and emotions have no outlet until we pause, making it more likely that you'll suddenly notice things you don't normally notice when you bring your attention to yourself.

- Use your best judgment: There is no need to stick with a practice if you're really overwhelmed by it. You can use your best judgment to decide whether to stick with a practice or to stop if you feel you are becoming overwhelmed by thoughts and emotions. You might also find that pain or other unpleasant physical sensations are louder with mindfulness practice, almost like a radio that has been turned up. You again always have the option to stop practicing, or use other ways to cope rather than mindfulness.
- *Redirecting your attention is not just a fancy way to avoid or stuff emotions down.* Our minds can be sneaky this way, so be aware if you might be using mindfulness practice to escape unpleasant feelings. Redirecting your attention from your mind to the "here and now" is simply an opportunity to say to yourself – "I'm getting really overwhelmed. I need to take a break and come back to this when I'm feeling calmer." This is a pretty important difference between pushing past or avoiding emotions, and instead intentionally making a decision to redirect depending on what you think you can manage at the time. Of course, the important part is that you do come back and reflect on what was going on for you in the moment, so you can attend to what was needed when you feel better equipped.
- Experiment: You won't always experience all practices the same way. If you are struggling with breathing, for example, you may want to avoid a mindful breathing exercise. It may be best to experiment with guided practices at first so you can become familiar with where your mind tends to go during meditation. It also gives you a built-in stopping point. You can always experiment with the length of time – some practices are as short as three minutes! – and then gradually working your way up to a longer period of practice. You can find guided examples of some of these practices in the online companion to this book.

**Practice Box 4.1 Mindfulness**

Try a mindfulness exercise – either formal, or informal, like a guided meditation. Jot down what you notice here.

# Part IV

# Adding to Your Toolbox

A broad set of strategies to manage the challenges that come alongside cancer.

# 5

# Making Space for Grief

It's impossible to talk about the experience of cancer without talking about grief. We normally associate the word "grief" with death. But really, grief is a normal response to any kind of important loss. And there is *so much* loss that can happen after a cancer diagnosis. Some of these losses might be obvious – like losing your hair, or a part of your body. Others are less visible – like losing the ability to think about the future without worrying about cancer, or loss of sexual intimacy.

These losses can feel even more intense if they're not recognized by others. There's actually a term for this – "disenfranchised grief."[1] Disenfranchised grief is grief that isn't acknowledged or supported by people in your life, or by society in general. It can also be grief that is misunderstood or minimized. There is such a powerful cultural message to focus on the "positive" with cancer that it can feel like you don't have permission to grieve what has been lost. It is sadly common to be told that you should be grateful for being alive, while truly devastating losses are dismissed. It's cruel and unfair. Any invalidation of your very real losses during cancer can lead to grief that feels like it has no outlet.[2,3]

When someone we care about has died, we have all of these ways to recognize and process that loss, like funeral services, writing a letter, or visiting a loved one's gravesite. These rituals give us a chance to feel our grief, instead of packing it away, unseen. Grief isn't meant to be hidden. It needs to be acknowledged so we don't get stuck in it. Because these rituals don't exist for losses that happen during cancer, this chapter will suggest some ideas for you to create some for yourself.

*Navigating Cancer: Research Supported Tools to Help You Cope with the Emotional and Physical Impact of Cancer*, First Edition. Jennifer Kilkus.  Published 2026 by John Wiley & Sons, Inc.
Companion Website: www.wiley.com/go/Kilkus/Navigatingcancer

**Reflection Box 5.1 Losses**

What losses have you experienced after your diagnosis? Have you been able to grieve your losses? If not, what has gotten in the way?

## Struggling in Quicksand

Grief can be really complicated, and there isn't a "right" way to handle it. It's so easy to get caught up in how things "used to be" before cancer. Or how things "should be" now.

Have you ever seen a movie or a television show where a character got stuck in quicksand? They panic – as most people would – and flail around trying to get out. Then what happens? *They get more stuck.* The more thrashing someone does in quicksand, the quicker and deeper they sink. The hero in the story eventually makes their way out by doing the opposite of what their instincts are telling them. They relax, slow down their movements to come to the surface, and then lay back to float on the surface. They can then safely and slowly get out. Struggling in our minds can be a lot like this. The more you wrestle with how things were before cancer, or how you think they should be now, the more you sink.

Which brings me back to that tough word I brought up in the last chapter – acceptance. To recap: Acceptance doesn't mean you have to be okay with what's happening. The hero in the quicksand isn't happy with their situation. They're probably terrified and exhausted. But they actually have to accept the situation before they can get themselves out of it. The more they struggle, the worse off they are. Accepting the reality means you can start to feel what needs to be felt. And with that, instead of being stuck, you can start to move through grief.

| Reflection Box 5.2 Wrestling with grief |
| --- |
| Are there any ways you have been wrestling with grief? What is keeping you stuck? |

## Honoring Stages of Grief

Accepting what has been lost is much easier said than done. It's worth noting the other emotions you may encounter as you navigate to acceptance. You might have heard of the "stages of grief."[2] This is a model that outlines the five most common emotions that come up during the mourning process: Denial, anger, bargaining, depression, and acceptance. This doesn't necessarily happen in a straight line: You might move back and forth through these different emotions. You could get to acceptance and then feel pulled into a different stage when a new challenge comes up. You might also skip all of these emotions and feel something else entirely. These stages just give you an idea of what to expect as you cope with what has been lost during cancer. Below, I've described these different stages. Take some time to reflect on what you've experienced and if any of these stages feel familiar to you.

**Denial:** This stage is often a first reaction to a loss. It can be protective, giving us time to truly understand that things won't go back to how they were. With denial, you might feel numb or like you're in shock. You might wonder if what has happened is a mistake, or find yourself fantasizing that they have diagnosed the wrong person. Denial can also look staying busy and distracted so you can dodge your feelings, or avoiding talking about what has happened, or acting like everything is okay even when it's not.

**Bargaining:** This may often look like "what if" or "if only" thinking. Bargaining is a way of trying to cope when you're experiencing emotional pain. You negotiate with yourself or with a higher power to feel like there is some way of going back to the way things were. "I'll do anything if only I could go back to life before cancer." Or, "If I had just gone to the doctor earlier, I wouldn't have had to get chemo." Or, "If I get through this, I'll never take life for granted again." It's an attempt to process a loss by fantasizing about scenarios that would be less painful.

**Anger:** Feeling angry is a completely normal response to a loss, but you might find it uncomfortable or challenging. As uncomfortable as it can be, anger may help us feel more in control instead of helpless. It gives a direction for anger, often in the form of blame. This could be blame toward yourself, or someone else, like a doctor or the medical system. It's also normal to feel angry at a higher power for allowing something so awful to happen. Guilt at feeling angry is common, making you feel even worse. At the heart of anger is hurt and pain. Recognizing and giving space to these hard emotions can help anger subside.

**Depression:** Hopelessness, feeling lost or confused, sadness, and lack of motivation are all a part of this stage of grief. Feeling depressed after a loss isn't the same thing as clinical depression – it's a normal response to facing the reality of a loss. It may be part of navigating grief, but it's also important to make sure you don't get overwhelmed by it. There are suggestions throughout the next chapters of the book to deal with these feelings so you don't get stuck in depression.

**Acceptance:** Being able to navigate loss in a healthy way means being able to get to a point where you learn to live with it. As I've mentioned before, accepting doesn't mean you're okay with what has happened. It just means that you are seeing reality as it is.

## Mourning Your Losses

There aren't any formal ways to mark losses during cancer, so it can be helpful to consider how you can create a way to do this for yourself. The purpose of this would be to allow yourself to acknowledge and feel whatever it is that you need to feel, so that you can move through the different stages that show up while grieving. This may take some time and experimentation to see what really feels like it connects for you. Whatever "ritual" you come up with doesn't have to be complicated. It can be as symbolic or straightforward as you want.

Maybe you just decide to clean out clothes that don't fit well anymore after a surgery, or ones that were your "comfort" clothes during treatment but now remind you of that difficult time. You can throw a "goodbye" or "retirement party" for your tumor, or burn any medical records or letters that have the word "cancer" on them. One of my clients painted painful words they associated with cancer on different sizes of rocks – the bigger the pain, the bigger the rock – and threw them off a bridge into a river.

You might also try writing as a way to move through grief. It can be as unfiltered as you want and include anything that you feel that you haven't been able to say out loud. You may even find it helpful to write a letter directly to whatever it is that you've lost – to say thank you, or to express anger, or sadness – whatever feels like it has been left unsaid. You can also decide you're not ready to face grief yet. That's perfectly okay. There is no timeline but your own, and you get to decide what feels manageable, and when.

**Reflection Box 5.3 Grief rituals**

Have you already completed any grief "rituals" related to cancer? How did it feel?

Are there other rituals you've tried in response to other losses you've had in your life? Could you try these with cancer too?

If not, are there any ideas that come to mind when thinking about memorializing cancer losses? Write them down here.

# 6

# Talking Back to That Voice in Your Head

We all talk to ourselves. Our mental chatter is such a huge part of our day-to-day experience that it might be hard to even picture what it would feel like to not think. Whether we're revisiting a conversation, commenting on something that is going on around us, or cooking up a future scenario to worry about, our minds are pretty much always working. Things get even busier up there when there is something going on that feels outside of our control. It can be absolutely *exhausting*. "*Why can't I shut my mind off?*" is a common question that I hear from people after a cancer diagnosis. It always leaves me wishing that there was some switch we had in the back of our heads to turn our minds off – or at least turn down the volume!

But usually, the problem isn't the thinking itself, but instead the "what" and the "how" of thinking. Our minds are *excellent* at making meaning out of situations. We come up with stories about stressful situations to make sense of them. Unfortunately, these stories may or may not always be accurate, and can have a big impact on how we feel emotionally. And since technology hasn't figured out a way to install that "off" switch, this chapter will give you some ideas on how to quiet the chatter.

## An Unfriendly Mind

Sometimes, the stories we tell ourselves about challenging situations are pretty unhelpful. We got into that a bit in the chapter on self-compassion – how those unhelpful thoughts can show up as a self-critical or unkind voice in our minds. But these unhelpful stories can play out in a lot of different ways.

Imagine a scenario that might be familiar to you: Waiting in a doctor's office. Picture it: You're in an uncomfortable chair, watching the minute hand tick by. Then the hour hand. Someone who arrives after you gets called back to the exam room. *What's going through your mind?*

Now – maybe you're a Zen master, and this wouldn't bother you at all. But, for the rest of us, it's easy to imagine what you might be thinking: *"I can't believe this!"; "This is so disrespectful!"; "I always have to wait HOURS"; "I feel awful, they should be more considerate!"; "Now I'm going to be late getting to day care pickup, and they charge extra when I'm late!"* And on and on – endless possibilities!

How would you guess someone having those thoughts might feel? Probably frustrated. Angry, even. Worried about being late. Maybe helpless. And that is completely understandable – it *is* an incredibly frustrating (and common!) experience. But if you have to be seen by the doctor, it's also out of your control. You can't change the situation.

So imagine the situation is the same, but what if you thought: "*Wow. They're really running behind. Maybe there's an emergency.*" You'd still be stuck in the waiting room, but maybe the emotions would shift – possibly to something less intense, or more accepting. You might even free up some space in your mind to problem solve – "*Maybe I'd better call the day care and let them know I'll be running late. Maybe they'll waive the fee this once.*"; "*Maybe Susan can pick her up.*"

The situation is the same. What has changed is your *interpretation* of it – the story you're telling yourself about it – and that can lead to a different emotional experience.

## Thinking and the Stress Response

We've gone over different ways thinking and behavior can influence how we feel physically, and how the stress response (*fight, flight, and freeze*) works in the body. We've also discussed that an essential first step in the activation of the stress response system is *assessment* – in other words, what we <u>think</u> about a situation tells the rest of our body what to do.[1] This can happen so quickly that it is not always a conscious process. Because of this, in highly emotional situations, our brains are more likely to rely on patterns for the sake of speed. These patterns are usually based on previous experiences and habits that are not always accurate or helpful for the current situation.

Assessing the situation is an essential step to help us cope. So what happens if a situation isn't an emergency, but we just *feel* like it is based on the patterns we've developed in our mind? The *fight, flight, freeze* response can get activated based on a faulty assessment, and continue on uninterrupted, developing more patterns that signal "danger" even if there aren't any right in this moment.[2] The theory behind cognitive behavioral therapy, and most other research-supported psychotherapies, is that our assessment of situations tends to be inaccurate and unhelpful when we are upset,[3] leading to a cycle of chronic reactivation of the *fight, flight, freeze* response that can become hard to interrupt. That's most likely to happen when we start to ruminate – that brooding, repetitive thinking that usually makes us feel awful and helpless, rather than helping us come up with any solutions.[4]

This gets tricky when we consider what happens with thinking following a diagnosis of cancer. Of course, it makes sense that most people assess this as a life-threatening situation, predictably triggering the stress response system. The challenge then becomes figuring out how to interrupt and redirect that system. While it is absolutely a normal reaction to respond to a cancer diagnosis and treatment as an emergency situation in your mind, it may not work in your body's best interest over time. Developing awareness of your habits in thinking and intentionally making efforts to shift them can go a long way to help quiet this system.

## Unhelpful Thinking

Your habits in thinking are developed over time. Like ways of coping, these habits usually start in childhood and get shaped by a few different things, including life experiences and what you may have observed other people doing around you. Let's say I grew up in a household where the family rule was to stay stoic and strong in response to challenges. If that was the only way I saw people handling tough situations, it would be left up to me to figure out how to cope that way. But what happens if I struggle? I might then assume that there's something "wrong" with me – that I'm weak, overly emotional, or not capable. Over time, this can develop into a habit of self-criticism and difficulty trusting myself to navigate challenges.

When we're distressed, we tend to think in ways that are biased and oversimplified. These types of thoughts are often our first, habitual, "knee-jerk" reaction to a situation, which is why in the cognitive behavioral therapy world they're called "automatic thoughts."[3] Automatic thoughts typically fall into predictable patterns. These patterns are known by a few different names, including cognitive distortions, thinking traps, and maladaptive thoughts. I prefer to refer to them as "unhelpful thinking patterns" – the other names feel critical to me. Given that we have little say in how these patterns develop and sometimes are not even aware of them, it seems unfair and ineffective to criticize ourselves for our thoughts (remember Chapter 3!). I think it is more useful to simply consider whether a particular thought is helpful or unhelpful for managing how you feel. Table 6.1 outlines a few pretty typical patterns of unhelpful thinking[3,5]:

**Table 6.1** Unhelpful thinking patterns.

| | |
|---|---|
| **All-or-nothing thinking:**<br>Seeing everything in black and white; only can see two ways of seeing things – "either/or" | "If I ask for help, I'm a failure."<br>"I can't walk as far as I used to, so why even try." |
| **Jumping to conclusions:**<br>• Mind reading: Imagining you know what others are thinking<br>• Fortune telling: Predicting the future | "I just know the test results are bad – the cancer's back."<br>"This pain will never get better."<br>"My partner hates my scars – that's why we haven't been intimate." |
| **Magnification (catastrophizing) or minimization:**<br>Blowing things out of proportion (magnification) or shrinking something inappropriately to make it seem less important | "If I have a mastectomy, my partner will leave me."<br>"My doctor has to be nice to me, they're probably telling me good news so I won't worry." |
| **Overgeneralization:**<br>Taking one instance in the past or present and apply to current or future situations | "My grandfather died of cancer; cancer is a death sentence."<br>"That medication didn't help at all, nothing is going to fix this." |
| **Emotional reasoning:**<br>Assuming that because you feel a certain way what you think must be true; if you felt more positively, you'd have a different perspective | I feel depressed, so "I might as well lie in bed all day"; "There's no point."<br>I feel fearful, so "This treatment isn't going to work." |

*(Continued)*

**Table 6.1** (Continued)

| | |
|---|---|
| **Personalization:** Blaming yourself or taking responsibility for something that wasn't completely your fault | "If I had eaten better, I wouldn't have gotten cancer." "There must be something wrong with me that I don't feel better yet." |
| **Labeling:** Assigning labels to yourself and other people | "I'm such a loser, I can't even get the dishes done anymore!" |
| **Shoulding/musting:** Applying critical words to ourselves and others that just create guilt, resentment, and frustration | "I shouldn't be struggling so much!" "Other people should know what I need." "I should be able to work a full day without being exhausted!" |

**Reflection Box 6.1 Recognize your thoughts**

Do you recognize any of your own thoughts in these unhelpful thinking styles? Make note of them here.

## The Pitfall of Positivity

Before I talk about how to manage these unhelpful ways of thinking, I need to get on my soapbox for a minute about positivity. You may have gotten the message that you need to stay positive or have a "fighting spirit" in response to cancer. This message can come from a lot of different places, including your family, or even your treatment team. Some people might even imply that your thinking could influence whether or not your treatment works or if you have a recurrence. **This is complete nonsense**. (I would use stronger language, but I'm trying to make this a clean book!). It's just an inaccurate, simplistic, and potentially even harmful way to view thinking around cancer.

Here's what's *actually* true: Yes, your thoughts can influence whether the *fight, flight, and freeze* response is activated. And yes, we know that this system, chronically activated over time, can impact your health more generally. **HOWEVER**, there is no definitive evidence that state-of-mind impacts cancer vulnerability, recovery, or recurrence. A whole body of research has been done over decades examining the link between personality traits, thoughts and attitudes, coping styles, and positive psychology states on different cancer outcomes. There is simply no evidence that "staying positive" will impact cancer.[6]

What's also true: Pressure to think positively can work in the exact opposite way as intended. It is difficult, if not impossible, to "will" ourselves into a different emotional state than the one that we are in. It's also counterproductive – emotions, when suppressed, have a way of rebounding and insisting on being felt anyway. When normal human emotions that one would expect to feel over the course of their cancer experience – like sadness, fear, grief, anger – are suppressed, it just ends up leading to more, and maybe even more intense, distress.[7] A former fellow I supervised lent me this metaphor: Imagine trying to hold down a beach ball under water. Eventually you get tired, or just want to get out of the pool. You let go, and the ball immediately rises to the surface. Emotions work the same way.

This doesn't mean that you can't try a coping skill to help yourself feel better, to mentally coach yourself when overwhelmed, or to do something like shift thinking toward what you are grateful for. It just means trying to *first* acknowledge and accept difficult thoughts and emotions rather than pushing them to the side. You can then make a deliberate choice to think in a way that is both validating and *balanced*, instead of either excessively positive or excessively negative.

**Reflection Box 6.2 Stay positive**

Has someone in your life encouraged you to "stay positive" as you navigate cancer? How did it make you feel?

Have *you* tried to think positively when you were struggling? Did it work? How did you feel afterward?

## How to Manage Unhelpful Thoughts: Reframing

Cognitive reframing is a foundational element of cognitive behavioral therapy (CBT)[3] that focuses on trying to find a different perspective with unhelpful thoughts. I mentioned earlier that when we're upset, we can think in ways that are biased – often toward the negative. Biased thinking also usually comes along with a whole boat load of assumptions that can make us feel worse instead of better. We can also easily "buy into" our thoughts, and see thoughts as absolute fact, instead of just a thought. The goal of cognitive reframing is to identify unhelpful thoughts, examine them, and replace them with thoughts that are more accurate or helpful.

Sometimes, the thoughts that you have are not biased or unrealistic. It might still be helpful to question your thinking, so to make sure there aren't any assumptions or exaggerations happening. But if your thoughts are realistic and accurate, it's best to use a different strategy other than reframing.

### Thought Tracking

Thought tracking, or a thought diary, is a strategy often used in CBT to start identifying habits in thought in response to specific situations. Below, in Table 6.2, is an example of a thought diary from Nic, who has recently been diagnosed with lymphoma.

**Table 6.2** Simple thought diary.

| Situation | Automatic Thought(s) | Emotions |
|---|---|---|
| Leaving the oncologist's office after she told me I have to have chemotherapy. | *"I'm never going to be able to get through this."*<br>*"I don't even know if this is going to work – the oncologist said I have a good chance but I'll probably just have to go through this and end up dying anyway!"*<br>*"There's no point!"*<br>*"I might as well do nothing so at least I'm not sick until I die!"* | Helpless<br>Scared<br>Angry |

Let's break each part of this down.

*Situation*: The situation can be something that happened or something you did (getting a scan result, having to see a friend for first time after losing your hair) or something that was more internal (a thought, an image or scenario that came in to your mind, a physical sensation, a flash back).

*Automatic Thought(s)*: When you notice your mood shift or that you're getting stuck in unhelpful thinking, try asking yourself: "*What was just going through my mind?*" to help you catch automatic thoughts. The automatic thought could be a thought, or it could show up in the form of a mental image. If you notice yourself including questions in the automatic thought column ("*Why is this happening to me?*"; "*Am I going to die?*"), try rephrasing the thought in the form of a statement ("*This shouldn't be happening to me*"; "*I'm afraid I'm going to die.*"). Thinking in the form of questions can get pretty circular, because there might not actually be an answer, or the answer doesn't reassure you. Phrasing it as a statement gives you an "off ramp" from circular thinking.

*Emotions*: Try to identify what emotion you felt the best you can. If you struggle to name emotions, this can be challenging. You can try starting with the basics: Sad, glad, mad, or afraid.

## What's the Evidence? Questioning Unhelpful Thoughts

A crucial piece of cognitive reframing is to evaluate how factual your thoughts are. As I mentioned earlier, this may be a challenge at first, since a lot of cancer-related unhelpful thoughts might have a kernel of truth to them. If you allow yourself to pause long enough to question your thoughts, however, there might be options to see where you can shift thinking in a direction that is more helpful. Here are a few questions you could try to ask yourself to start to find more flexibility in thinking:

> *What makes me think this thought is true? What facts do I have to support it?* (Remember to be honest with yourself here, and try to truly include facts, not feelings!).

Going back to Nic's example, what facts do you see there to support their unhelpful thoughts? They are correct that no one knows what the outcome of the treatment will be. Their other thoughts don't seem to have any facts that are supporting them.

*What makes me think this thought isn't true, or maybe not 100% true? Are there any facts that support that this thought is not true?*

Nic mentions that their oncologist said that they have a "good chance." We don't have any more information than that, but Nic could certainly ask their oncologist specifics about this so they can have more facts that help them better understand the likelihood of the treatment being effective. Nic also says they will "never make it through this." We can probably assume this is not 100% true, as many people receive chemotherapy treatment for lymphoma, and while of course it *is* really rough, there is a good chance Nic can get through it.

*Am I thinking about things in "all-or-nothing" terms, or using exaggerated words or phrases like "always," "never," "should," "must," or "can't?"*

This one is pretty straight forward. We can see that Nic is having a hard time imagining a future where they made it through treatment and it helped. They are thinking in absolutes and having a hard time imagining alternatives.

*Are my thoughts based on feelings rather than facts? If I were feeling a different way, would I see this situation differently?*

Nic is very likely filtering thoughts through the emotions they are experiencing. If they were feeling calmer, it is easier to imagine that they might be able to have a more balanced perspective.

*Are there any other ways of seeing this situation? What would I say to a friend or someone I love who was in the same situation?*

While it completely makes sense that Nic is feeling fearful and helpless, their thoughts are probably feeding those emotions. If they were talking to a friend, they might encourage them that although it will be hard, they can make it through. Or that while we don't know the outcome of the treatment, it is the best chance they have to survive their disease.

*What is this way of thinking costing me, emotionally or practically?*

In this case, Nic's thoughts are probably making them feel worse. It's also costing time – their worry is taking up the only time they can truly live in: *here and now*. In an extreme case, their thoughts may actually cause them to avoid treatment, which could become life-threatening.

*Is this truly the most helpful way to think about this?*

Often, this is an obvious answer. Even so, just asking the question is a cue that there may be other ways of thinking about even the most challenging situations. The trick is in the "how," which I'll discuss next.

## Helpful Thinking: Alternative Thoughts

After some practice with challenging unhelpful thinking, the next step is to start to develop more helpful, balanced, and realistic thoughts that can replace them – in CBT, these are called "alternative thoughts." Alternative thoughts take the information that was gathered in the questioning process and use it to develop a replacement thought that is less likely to continue triggering more negative thoughts and emotions.

When developing alternative thoughts, it can be helpful to incorporate the concept of "**both/and**" to manage what can often feel like two seemingly opposite thoughts or emotions. "Both/and" is borrowed from a type of modified CBT called dialectical behavior therapy (DBT). We talked about a skill from DBT in Chapter 4. "Dialectic" means squaring ideas or feelings that seem like they are opposite to each other, or contradict each other. Working with a dialectic means getting away from "either/or" way of thinking toward something that is more flexible – "both/and."[8] Take a look at a longer version of the thought diary that includes some possible alternative thoughts that Nic can use in Table 6.3.

Next, let's try an example using a common scenario that occurs during cancer treatment: Fatigue.

John has a history of prostate cancer. He had both radiation treatment and androgen deprivation therapy, and while grateful that there is no evidence of remaining cancer, he's really struggling with fatigue. He spends most of his time watching TV. He's avoiding spending time with his grandchildren because he's so tired and worried he won't be able to keep up anymore. Below, in Table 6.4, see if you might be able to identify

**Table 6.3** Thought diary with alternative thoughts.

| Situation | Automatic Thought(s) | Emotions | Unhelpful Thinking Patterns | Alternative Thoughts |
|---|---|---|---|---|
| Leaving the oncologist's office after she told me I have to have chemotherapy. | *"I'm never going to be able to get through this."* | Helpless<br>Scared<br>Angry | All-or-nothing thinking | *"I know this will be hard and I'm scared, but I can get through this with the support of my friends."* |
| | *"I don't even know if this is going to work – the oncologist said I have a good chance but I'll probably just have to go through this and end up dying anyway!"* | | Jumping to conclusions | *"It's normal for me to be scared; anyone would be in this situation."* |
| | *"There's no point!"* | | Emotional reasoning | *"I don't know if the treatment will work, but the oncologist thinks I have a good chance and it's the best option I have to get rid of the cancer."* |
| | *"I might as well do nothing so at least I'm not sick until I die!"* | | Magnification | *"I still have a lot I want to do in life and I'll need this treatment to make sure I can do them."* |
| | | | | *"I don't know how sick I'll get but I'm willing to try treatment so I have the best possible chance of surviving."* |

the unhelpful thinking patterns John is using and possible alternative thoughts to help him shift his thinking.

**Table 6.4** John's thought diary.

| Situation | Automatic Thought(s) | Emotions | Unhelpful Thinking Patterns | Alternative Thoughts |
|---|---|---|---|---|
| My daughter called and asked if she could bring the kids over for a few hours. | *"I'm too exhausted, I'll never be able to keep up!"*<br>*"I don't want them to know how useless I've become – this isn't me."*<br>*"They don't want to spend time with someone who just lays on the couch all the time."* | Sad<br>Frustrated<br>Tired | | |

Now, in Table 6.5, try using cognitive reframing with a recent stressful situation you've had.

**Table 6.5** Blank thought diary.

| Situation | Automatic Thought(s) | Emotions | Unhelpful Thinking Patterns | Alternative Thoughts |
|---|---|---|---|---|
| | | | | |

## How to Manage Unhelpful Thoughts: Coaching Yourself

In Chapter 3, I mentioned how important it is to be able to speak to ourselves in a more compassionate, encouraging way. This can be really useful for stopping the spiral of unhelpful thoughts. That might be particularly true for thoughts where there is simply no other way to think about the situation. You're not catastrophizing, or imagining a worst-case scenario. Maybe you already are dealing with the worst-case scenario, like having heard the news that your cancer has spread, or that the treatment isn't working. Or maybe the thing you're worried about has a good possibility of happening, like the chance of recurrence.

These are tough, real situations that can come up during cancer, and you may not be thinking about it in a way that reframing can help. In that case, the trick would be to redirect your thoughts to more encouraging, coaching types of thoughts instead. I outlined some options in the chapter on self-compassion, but to recap, you'll want to find something that sounds supportive and encouraging. You're not getting into the "facts," you're just trying to think of something that can help calm you or interrupt panic. It's worth saying again that this doesn't have to be positive – in fact, that might actually make you feel worse. For example, if you said to yourself "Everything will be okay" when you're not sure if it actually will be okay, it probably won't help all that much. Our brains know when we're not really buying into something.

This is really personal, and it may take some trial and error to find the right words, but here are some examples:

- I'm stronger than I think.
- I'm still here.
- I can take things one step at a time.
- Everything is temporary.

| **Reflection Box 6.3 Coaching statements** |
|---|
| Do any coaching statements come to mind? Are there encouraging things you've said to yourself in the past that might be helpful in this situation, too? |

7

# Working with Your Body

Have you ever had a few nights of bad sleep and ended up snapping at someone for no real reason? Or maybe, like me, you have a hard time being reasonable when you're hungry. The times I have not been my best self have always been when I was too tired or hungry (*and my deepest apologies to anyone who has experienced me when both are happening at the same time*). It's much harder to cope emotionally when there is a lot happening to your body physically, and of course, the physical impact of cancer and cancer treatment are *way* more intense than missing just one night of sleep. There is an onslaught of things that your body might experience during treatment – hair loss, surgery, radiation burns, IVs... Your body can start to feel totally out of your control. This chapter is all about introducing ways to help calm both your body and your mind. These skills are meant to work *with* your body to help you feel a little more in control.

## The Mind–Body Connection

Our minds are incredibly good at influencing our bodies. We started by talking about the biopsychosocial model, which highlights how health and well-being are influenced by what's happening in your mind and your environment. The placebo effect is a perfect illustration of this. You may have heard of a placebo before, but if you're not the kind of person who reads clinical trials in their spare time, you might not know exactly

*Navigating Cancer: Research Supported Tools to Help You Cope with the Emotional and Physical Impact of Cancer*, First Edition. Jennifer Kilkus.  Published 2026 by John Wiley & Sons, Inc.
Companion Website: www.wiley.com/go/Kilkus/Navigatingcancer

what it is. A placebo is some kind of substance, like a pill, an injection, or some other type of medical treatment that has no active ingredient. Placebos are used in clinical trials to compare the actual treatment being tested against a treatment with no active ingredient.[1] Sometimes, people who get the placebo still have an improvement – even when they're getting a fake treatment. This is called a placebo effect.[2] Researchers have found that this can even work in the opposite direction, called a nocebo effect. The nocebo effect happens when a placebo causes a negative outcome even when there is no active treatment being given.[1,2]

So what is going on here? It's the powerful influence of the mind on the body – a psychological process that influences how the body reacts. Researchers who study placebo and nocebo think that there are two main causes of this – learning and expectation.[3] Our brains are incredible at making associations. If we feel an improvement in pain after taking a placebo, for example, it may be because we've learned in the past that taking a medication for pain reduces our pain. Another possible cause of the placebo effect is the power of our expectations. If we expect that a medication will help – or the opposite, if we think it won't, or that it will hurt us – that expectation makes a difference in how our body responds. This also can be influenced by other people around us, too. For example, if a researcher in a clinical trial suggests that they're confident the treatment will work, a participant will be more likely to have a positive response to a placebo.[3] The precise *how* of this is still a bit fuzzy in the research, but studies suggest that the placebo and nocebo effect can be explained by a series of changes that happen in the parts of the brain that are related to pain processing and emotion management.[3,4] For example, an expectation that a pain medication will work, even if you receive a placebo, can cause an increase in endorphins, the body's natural pain relievers.

The stress response system also plays a role in the mind–body connection. When we interpret a situation as threatening, our stress response system gets activated. Stress hormones, like cortisol and epinephrine, are released to circulate in the body, our muscles get tense, and our heart rate and blood pressure will go up,[5] and all of that activity in the body can make physical symptoms feel more intense. To make matters worse, any kind of unpleasant physical experience, like pain or feeling sick, can be viewed as a threat in our minds – "*I can't believe I'm in pain again, will this ever stop?*" – and then that activates the stress response system. Over time, your body starts to learn this connection, and it becomes a cycle. It starts with you being in pain, followed by activation of the stress response system, and then that activation worsens pain. Once that connection has been made, you might be more likely to start *expecting* pain, causing the stress response system to be activated even in the absence of pain, which may then trigger or intensify an episode of pain.[4] Just like with the placebo effect, that ability for our brains to *learn* associations and our *expectations* again can change what happens in the body. So being able to work with the mind–body connection to interrupt this cycle can go a long way in helping to manage the impact of cancer and cancer treatment.

## Rest and Digest

So far, I've been really focused on the stress response system – *fight*, *flight*, and *freeze*. What I haven't mentioned is that this is just one part of your autonomic nervous system called the *sympathetic nervous system*. The other part is your *parasympathetic nervous system*, also known as *rest* and *digest* – the counterbalance to *fight*, *flight*, and *freeze*. The parasympathetic nervous system controls your body's ability to relax and keeps your day-to-day maintenance processes like your resting heart rate, your digestion, and your metabolism steady.[5] Similar to how our minds can activate the *fight*, *flight*, and *freeze* system, we can also activate the *rest* and *digest* system. The exercises included in the rest of this chapter are different ways to help yourself shift from a stressed state to a more relaxed one by tapping into the parasympathetic nervous system.

Learning to influence the parasympathetic nervous system can be helpful in a lot of scenarios you might be experiencing after a diagnosis, including coping with pain, feeling anxious or overwhelmed, insomnia, or feeling disconnected from your body. With practice, you can get better at noticing when you're in *fight*, *flight*, or *freeze*, and develop more control over calming your body in the moment. These exercises have been studied for decades, including with people navigating cancer, and there is a solid foundation of evidence of the benefits for a long list of different health outcomes like reduction of anxiety and stress, headaches, hypertension, sleep quality, pain, fatigue, nausea, and more.[6–17] You may not find every one of these exercises helpful in the same way, but I hope you'll find one or two that leave you feeling better in your body.

## Before Getting Started

- *Do not do anything that causes pain.* These types of exercises are **not** a "no pain, no gain" situation. The hope is that you feel better physically and emotionally afterward, not worse. If there is any instruction that causes you pain, feel free to ignore it or stop the exercise. Be cautious if you've recently had a surgery or have any areas in your body that are tender and use your best judgment. If you've recently had a surgery on your lung for example, the diaphragmatic breathing exercise is probably one to avoid for now.
- Because these exercises can lower your blood pressure and heart rate, take it slow when you're standing up afterward. If you feel lightheaded, stop the exercise and take a few minutes breathing at your normal pace.
- Just like with mindfulness practice, you might find these exercises challenging to focus on. Most people aren't in the habit of being quiet and focusing on their body, so there is a lot of potential for your mind to become more aware of discomfort. It will likely pass, and you can use the exercise to distract your mind from whatever discomfort you're feeling. You might also just find that your mind bounces around a lot. This is not a problem: Make a note of it, and then practice shifting your attention back to the steps of the exercise.
- Again, like with mindfulness practice, you may find it most helpful to listen to a recorded guided exercise – it can be hard to juggle both reading the steps and trying to follow them at the same time. You can find recordings of the exercises below in the online companion to this book.

## Progressive Muscle Relaxation

Progressive muscle relaxation, or PMR, is an active relaxation technique that was first developed in the 1930s.[6] PMR is a practice that focuses on deliberately tensing and holding the tense muscle for several seconds, and then relaxing. It's called "progressive" because it starts with the major muscle groups throughout the body, starting at the head and working down, or starting at the toes and working up. The process of deliberately tensing the muscle and then relaxing it signals the body to shift from the *fight*, *flight*, and *freeze* state into *rest* and *digest*. As muscle tension drops, other areas that are activated by the stress response system, like heart rate and blood pressure, drop too. As you practice, you'll also get quicker at noticing the difference between when your muscles are tense and when they're relaxed, so that you can adjust before the tension starts causing you trouble.

In my work, I've noticed that some people struggle with tensing their muscles – either because it causes them pain or a muscle spasm, or they don't feel they have the strength to squeeze them tightly. If you have trouble with the tensing part of the instruction, you can still benefit from intentionally relaxing the muscle and trying to feel heavy in your body. The tensing gives you a "running start" to signal the stress response system, but it's not required to feel more relaxed. You might find it useful to experiment with both and see what you prefer.

To start PMR, get into a comfortable position. Make sure your legs and ankles are uncrossed and your hands are resting on your thighs or a piece of furniture, with your hands open and fingers relaxed. You might find it easiest to lay down on a bed or a couch with pillows propping you up comfortably, so you don't need to use any muscle tension to hold yourself up. Once you're settled, take the following steps:

- Starting with your forehead, inhale and raise your eyebrows as high as you can and hold for 5 seconds. Exhale and relax for 10 seconds.
- Moving on to your upper cheeks and nose: Inhale and squint your eyes and wrinkle up your nose as tense and tight as you can for 5 seconds. Again, exhale and relax for 10 seconds.
- Next, clench your teeth and push your tongue against the back of your teeth. Hold for 5 seconds. Relax for 10. Pause and just notice how your face and jaw feel.
- Now, moving to the neck and shoulders. Try to tighten your neck muscles by lowering your chin. Hold for 5 seconds, then breathe out and relax for 10. Raise your shoulders up to your ears, while also tightening between your shoulder blades. Hold for 5, then exhale and relax.
- Noticing now your abdomen and lower back. Inhale and squeeze your abdominal muscles and lower back as tight as you can. Hold for 5 seconds, exhale and relax. Again take a few seconds here to just notice how your body is feeling. Are there any differences between your upper body and your lower body?

- Moving on to your lower body now. Inhale and clench and squeeze your glute muscles in your seat. Hold for 5 seconds, exhale, and relax for 10 seconds.
- Now do the same for both your upper leg muscles. Inhale and squeeze as tight as you can, hold for 5 seconds, then exhale and relax for 10.
- Next, noticing your calf muscles, and with an inhale, squeezing those as tight as you can, hold for 5 seconds, and relaxing again for 10.
- Finally with your feet – clench your toes as tight as you can while also pointing your toes downward. Hold for 5 seconds, then relax for 10.

Now just allow yourself to take a few minutes and notice how your body feels.

| **Reflection Box 7.1 Relaxation reflection** |
|---|
| What did you notice about this exercise?<br><br><br>Were there any muscles that were particularly tense? Was it challenging to get them to relax?<br><br><br>Did any muscles relax when you were paying attention to them, but then tense again once you moved your attention away? |

## Diaphragmatic Breathing

Diaphragmatic breathing is a great exercise to do on its own or to add on to a PMR exercise. Your diaphragm is a muscle that sits below your lungs and supports your breathing. It flattens when you inhale and relaxes when you exhale. The diaphragm is one of the most efficient muscles in the body and allows you to use 100% of your lung capacity to breathe. We all breathe diaphragmatically when we're born. If you have ever seen a baby breathe, you've probably noticed that their belly moves up and down as they breathe. That's the diaphragm doing its job. As we age, and when we're under stress, we get into the habit of breathing faster and shallower, using more of our neck and chest muscles to breathe. This not only keeps us from breathing fully, but it also causes neck and shoulder tension.

Breathing diaphragmatically allows your body to exchange oxygen and carbon dioxide at the right ratios to prevent hyperventilation. Hyperventilation happens when you breathe too deeply or too quickly, and it leads to you not having enough carbon dioxide in your blood. Breathing diaphragmatically encourages your body to stop taking in too much oxygen when you breathe in so your body can re-regulate the amount of carbon dioxide that's in your blood. When you breathe from your diaphragm, your breathing rate is slower, your blood pressure and heart rate is lower, and you can lower the amount of stress hormones in your body. In short, it's a quick way to activate the *rest* and *digest* system. There are a lot of different types of breathing exercises that you may have run across like "box" breathing, 4-7-8 breathing, alternate nostril breathing, or others. It can get really confusing to figure out what the "right" type of breathing is. *Any* type of breathing exercise that feels comfortable and relaxing is good. There is no one "perfect" way to breathe, other than to aim to use the muscle that is designed to carry the weight of your breathing – your diaphragm. That being said, as I mentioned earlier in the chapter, you might be challenged to use your diaphragm to breathe because of the cancer or a treatment you've had. Just do your best to breathe comfortably and don't push to do anything that doesn't feel comfortable.

To get started, you'll want to get in a comfortable position similar to what I suggested for PMR. You might find it helpful to put one hand on your chest and one hand on your belly so you can notice where your breathing is coming from.

- Inhale slowly in from your nose. Your belly should rise as you breathe in, like a balloon inflating. You want the hand on your belly to rise, and the hand on your chest to stay about the same.

- Breathe out slowly, allowing your belly to flatten like a deflating balloon.
- Before inhaling again, you'll want to pause for a few seconds. The pause is not to hold your breath – it's just to be still and relax.
- If at any time you begin to feel lightheaded or dizzy, you are exchanging too much air. Either return to your normal breathing pattern, or better, wait longer between breaths and do not breathe as deeply.
- Start with 5 minutes, and as you get more comfortable, build up 1 or 2 minutes at a time. How long you practice is up to you, but a good target would be 10–15 minutes two times per day. You can also practice any time you are feeling physically or emotionally uncomfortable. You can do an adapted version of this practice while sitting or standing, so it's a practice that will always be available to you wherever you are.

**Reflection Box 7.2 Breathing reflection**

What did you notice about this exercise? Include any observations here, including anything that felt challenging or uncomfortable.

## Guided Imagery

Guided imagery is a type of focused relaxation that uses your imagination to create calm, positive images in your mind. It uses your imagination to create a mental picture that includes all of your senses – vision, taste, touch, smell, and sound – to put yourself in a calmer state. Sometimes, when your body is going through a lot, you may not feel like a body-based exercise is helpful. In that case, you can use the power of the mind–body connection to bring yourself somewhere in your mind that may feel safer than focusing your attention on your body. Guided imagery has the same benefits on the body as PMR and diaphragmatic breathing, so if those exercises don't suit you, this one might.

**Practice Box 7.1 Lemon exercise**

Imagine that you're in a kitchen, looking at a bright yellow lemon sitting on a cutting board. Picture yourself picking up the lemon and holding its weight in your hand. Feel its knobbly, waxy texture across your fingertips. Now imagine picking up a knife and cutting that lemon in half and holding it up to your nose. Imagine the sharp and fresh scent. Now picture biting into the sour, juicy pulp.

What did you notice as you pictured this scene? Did your mouth pucker or water? Did you notice your stomach grumbling, or your salivary glands start to activate?

Such a great example of how our imagination can cause changes in our body that can be immediate and noticeable.

There are so many different options for practicing guided imagery that the options are limitless. You can envision one of your most happy memories in as much detail as you can. You can also use images of nature to put yourself in a calmer place, like imagining a favorite place you've been, or picturing being at a calm beach or a tranquil forest scene. Some guided imagery exercises have you picture your body from inside out, with all of your internal systems working together to help you heal. I'll include an imagery here that allows you to create your own peaceful place, but I'd encourage you to explore different options to see what you might connect with best.

To start this imagery, get yourself as comfortable as you can. Use anything you need to help support your body, like pillows or blankets.

Begin by breathing normally. Just noticing how your body feels as you breathe slowly in and out.

As you breathe, see if you can start to allow your body to become heavy. Just letting your body sink into whatever you're sitting or lying on.

Now bring to mind a place where you feel completely relaxed and peaceful. This may be somewhere you have been before, or it may be a place that you've created in your mind.

Where is this place? Is it inside, or outside? Small, or large? Cozy, or a wide-open space?

What kind of place do you need to feel completely relaxed?

Who is around you? Are you alone, or with someone you love? Are there any animals around, like a beloved pet, or birds chirping? Remember, this can be whatever you want it to be, so this can include people or animals that are no longer with you.

What sounds can you hear? Try to imagine in as much detail as you can.

What's the temperature like? Cool, or warm? Is there a breeze, or is the air calm and still?

What else can you picture? What colors make up this landscape you've created? What objects are around you? Are there parts of the natural world, like plants or a stream? Or maybe more of the world inside, like a cracking fireplace, or a cozy chair?

What are you doing in this place? Maybe absolutely, gloriously, nothing. Or maybe you're walking. Reading. Stretching. Doing something that helps you to feel calm, soothed.

Imagine a feeling of peace coming over you. Nothing to do. Nowhere to go. No one to be, but just you, here. In a place where you can truly let go and relax.

Now, just take a few minutes and let yourself be in this calm place you created for yourself.

Whenever you're ready, you can move on to the rest of your day, trying to bring some of that sense of calm with you.

**Reflection Box 7.3 Peaceful place**

Take a mental picture of the peaceful place you created. What pieces of it were most calming for you?

Could you recreate this again?

When would be the best time for you to create this peaceful place?

Are there any challenges to continuing to practice this exercise?

## Self-soothing

Sometimes, you may just need a quick strategy that can bring you comfort. Self-soothing focuses on using your five senses to help yourself feel calmer or more relaxed. These are things that we think of automatically when caring for a small child – comforting them with a teddy bear or a fuzzy blanket, or playing soothing music. For whatever reason, we forget that as adults, we need soothing, too. Using your senses to take care of yourself combines two powerful tools – mindfulness, and tapping into your parasympathetic nervous system. It is also usually a strategy that you can use anywhere – whether you're at home, in a hospital bed, or waiting to see the oncologist.

*Touch:* What kind of physical sensations would feel comforting to you? Maybe you have a favorite set of cozy pajamas, or really like the feel of freshly washed sheets. What about giving yourself a short hand massage, or even just wrapping your arms around yourself, like a hug? Touch can also include temperature, which can be so powerful for working with your nervous system. If you're feeling down and in need of comfort, a hot bath may help. If you're feeling agitated or anxious, you would go for colder temperatures – an ice pack on your face, a cool shower, or having a fan blow on your skin.

*Sight:* Are there any images you associate with calm? I live near the sea in Ireland, and many of the people I work with find the images of waves going in and out to be soothing. Or maybe imagining your children playing is more useful, or possibly the image of someone you consider to be calm or resilient. Anything that feels like it might help you ground yourself.

*Sounds:* There are so many choices with sound – do you need lifting up? Maybe that means listening to fun, energetic music. Calming down? Classical music, ocean noises, bird song – this can be really personal. You might need to experiment a bit to see what fits for you, and it can help to be prepared by having a playlist already put together that you can have at the ready.

*Smells:* This can be a tricky one during active treatment because your sensitivity to smells may have changed. So go carefully, but see if you can find some smells that are soothing – a favorite shampoo, candle, or flower – that you can keep nearby.

*Taste:* Similar to smell, taste can be a moving target during treatment. Do you have a favorite special treat? Or is there something that feels soothing to eat simply because it doesn't make you feel sick? Maybe a hot tea or some other type of hot drink could also feel good to try.

**Practice Box 7.2 Five senses**

Choose one of the five senses and find something that you think might comfort you. Make a mental note of how you feel before and after.

Did it seem to help, even if was briefly? If not, keep trying – it can take some time to find what feels best.

# 8

# Pacing Yourself

It is not news to anyone reading this book that figuring out the "sweet spot" of rest and activity during and after cancer treatment is a moving target. What you want to do and what your body feels capable of doing can sometimes be completely different things. That can make it really complicated to figure out when you need to take it easy and when you might need to push yourself. Recovery can take much longer than you expect, which of course is incredibly frustrating when you just want to feel "normal" again. Because treatments for cancer can be so impactful, falling on either side of too much or too little activity can have long-lasting consequences for your mood and energy level. This chapter focuses on helping you try to strike the right balance and offers some strategies for helping yourself either slow down or ramp up depending on what you might need.

## Hitting the Brakes

Kim finished 6 weeks of radiation treatment about two months ago. She's climbing up the walls at this point – she's tired of being tired and can't wait to get out of the house and *do* something. Most days, though, she's finding it hard to do much of anything at all. This is *infuriating* for Kim, who is used to working a full-time job, running her kids to all their activities, and playing in a recreational softball team on the weekends.

She finds herself getting into a pattern – she has a "good" energy day, and then spends the whole day going "all out." She sees some friends

*Navigating Cancer: Research Supported Tools to Help You Cope with the Emotional and Physical Impact of Cancer*, First Edition. Jennifer Kilkus.  Published 2026 by John Wiley & Sons, Inc.
Companion Website: www.wiley.com/go/Kilkus/Navigatingcancer

for lunch, does some grocery shopping, and tries to do a few hours of work from home. She's still feeling good in the evening, so she goes to the park with her family. But the next day she is completely wrecked. She can barely get out of bed and counts it as a success if she can get herself in the shower. Over time, she's finding that these "good" energy days are few and far in between, and she's having more days when she's feeling tired. She thinks, "*Shouldn't I be getting better the further away from treatment I am? What's wrong with me?*"

Does any of Kim's story sound familiar to you? This is called the "boom-bust" cycle of activity and is pretty common when people are trying to find the right level of activity during and after treatment. This cycle was identified in the fields of chronic pain and chronic fatigue,[1,2] but researchers have found this "boom-bust" cycle also happens during cancer treatment and recovery from treatment.[3,4] The cycle happens when people repeatedly push themselves beyond their max when they have something going on physically that makes it difficult for them to recover. Over time, that can start to drain the body's ability to recover even further. As seen in Figure 8.1, fatigue or pain worsens, limiting activity even more, and it becomes harder and harder to bounce back.

It's kind of like how inflation works. (Stick with me, I promise this makes sense!) With inflation, the price of everyday things get more expensive because of increased demand or lower supply. Wages usually don't keep up with inflation as it rises. So as time goes on, we find ourselves in a position where everything costs more, but we have the same amount of money in the bank. That money doesn't go as far as it used

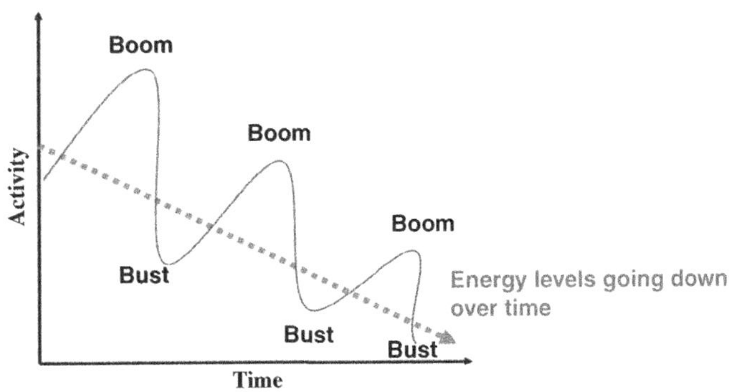


**Figure 8.1** Energy levels in a "boom-bust" cycle.

to. Now imagine that you start to use credit cards to cover the gap of what you can buy. The interest on the credit cards means that ultimately things cost even more, and it becomes even harder to pay your bills. That's what "boom-bust" is like. Every time you push beyond your max when you're recovering, you're spending "money" that you don't have, and are getting into an energy or pain "debt."

It can be so discouraging to be stuck in this cycle when all you want is to feel like yourself again. Luckily, there are some things you can do to support your recovery in a more sustainable way.

## Activity Pacing

Activity pacing is a strategy that can interrupt the "boom-bust" cycle and help improve worsening fatigue or pain that comes from being stuck in this cycle.[5] Activity pacing has two main priorities:

1. Conserving energy for activities that are important to you
2. Planning and pacing your activity so high demand activities are mixed with lower demand activities and periods of rest.

### What Is Draining You?

Activity pacing requires you to pay close attention to yourself so that you can get familiar with what activities drain you the most. "Activity" doesn't just include what you're doing physically. Activities that are emotionally demanding or use a lot of brain power can be just as draining. You might find it helpful to temporarily let go of activities that cost a lot of energy but don't give a lot back. An example of this would be using your limited energy to clean the house and then not having energy left to spend time with people you care about.

Tracking this over time can be incredibly useful for getting a handle on which activities drain your energy the most. Once you have a sense of what activities are most draining, you can start to plan around "high demand" activities.

Let's look at Kim's day again. If she takes a critical eye to her activities, she'd probably admit that there are some pretty draining ones in her day. Even though she really wants to see her friends *and* go with her family to the park, that's a lot of social activity for her – something that drained her tank pretty fast even before cancer. Work also seems like it's more tiring than it used to be. Concentrating for a few hours at a time can really be exhausting for her. Grocery shopping isn't particularly draining for her, but it takes more effort when it's combined with everything else.

### What's the Priority?

Deciding what the high priority activities are each day is essential to pacing effectively. It's easy to get stuck in the *should* – "I *should* be able to do all of these things in one day, I used to be able to!" – and not focus on the reality. For Kim, right now she has to prioritize doing some work each day. She took a lot of time off for cancer treatment, and is working with her employer to slowly build back up to full-time. Her family has been managing, but they could really use her income. The rest is a bit harder to figure out how to prioritize, but if she absolutely had to choose, she would choose to spend time with her family.

### Hitting the Brakes Before You "Hit the Wall"

Now that Kim has a better idea of what's draining her energy the most, and what the priority activities are, she can bring her attention to any "warning signs" she might be getting about her energy level. She describes feeling like she "hits a wall" in the day, where she feels like her energy is totally gone. This usually happens in the early afternoon, and sometimes she notices that she has more trouble concentrating or finding her words before then. She usually gets more irritable around this time, too.

### Planning and Adapting

Activity pacing is all about using what you learn about your body and what it needs to plan your activity in a strategic way. Kim's reality is that she can't continue to do all the same activities she used to do in the same way she used to do them without getting into the "boom-bust" cycle. But now that she has a little more data, she can start to plan more effectively.

If Kim had a "do-over" of her good energy day to build one that was better paced, she'd do it a little differently. Because her priorities are to work and to spend time with her family, she'd stick to just those activities for one day. She'd still have a meal with her friends, because that's important too, but would plan it for a day where she wasn't working. She might decide to try for breakfast instead of lunch since that's the time of day she has more energy. Her paced day would also include resting in the afternoon, when she's starting to "hit a wall." Groceries could be done by her partner, or by a family friend who has been offering to do tasks around the house. She has noticed that she seems to do better if she can break work down into shorter "bursts" and plans three one-hour blocks to work alternating with activities that don't require much concentration to give herself a break.

**Reflection Box 8.1 Hit the wall**

Think back to the last day you had when you may have "hit the wall." Were there opportunities to pace yourself? What would a "do-over" look like so that you could have a more balanced day?

## Pressing on the Gas

We're going to head in the opposite direction now and focus on how to get moving again if you're feeling stuck. Getting stuck can happen for a lot of different reasons – feeling down or depressed, avoidant coping, the physical impact of cancer treatments, or getting weaker over time because you haven't been able to move much because of cancer or cancer treatments. Like a lot of things while navigating cancer, this is a pretty classic biopsychosocial problem. Feeling unwell physically leads to doing less, doing less leads to fewer positive experiences, fewer positive experiences leads to feeling down and unmotivated, making it even harder to do more. Sometimes, this can even lead to physical deconditioning. Physical deconditioning is what happens after our bodies go through an extended period of inactivity, like after an injury or illness. Your body starts to adapt to not having as many physical demands, causing muscle loss and weakness.[6] That can make it even harder to get back to activity.

Figure 8.2 outlines what this process looked like for Tyler. Tyler is recovering from an intense bout of treatment for testicular cancer including surgery and chemotherapy. He's exhausted all the time even

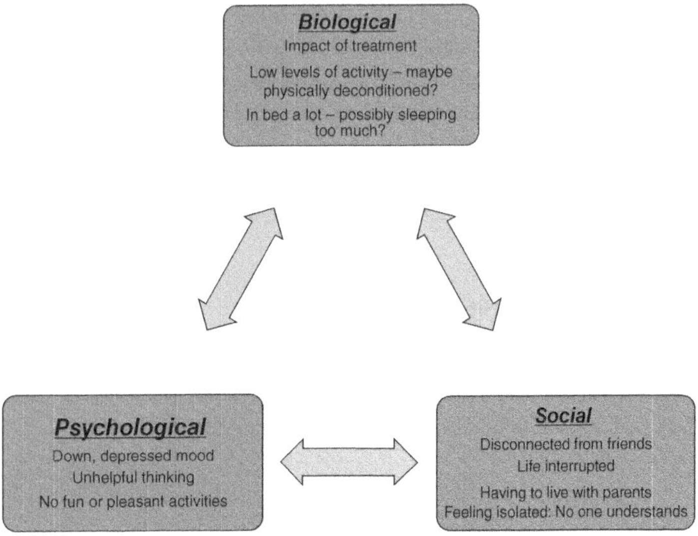


**Figure 8.2** A biopsychosocial look at Tyler's challenges.

though he sleeps at least 12 hours every day, and he hasn't really been able to get moving again. He had to move back in to live with his parents during treatment (*not* something he was thrilled about in his 20s!) and spends most of his time in his room in bed on his laptop. All of his friends are busy with work or school, so he hasn't been seeing much of them. He feels like they can't really understand what he's going through, anyway, and doesn't want to be seen as a "cancer patient." He finds himself thinking "*What's the point?*" a lot and doesn't know how to move forward from here.

## Behavioral Activation

There are a lot of different things going on for Tyler, but a big part of what is keeping him stuck is how disengaged he is with his life. And it makes sense – he's still struggling physically, and his whole life has been turned upside down. But if something doesn't change, he'll just continue to get more and more stuck.

Behavioral activation is a cognitive behavioral therapy strategy that focuses on trying to do more over time to feel better.[7] It focuses on making manageable, small changes over time to interrupt the cycle of feeling stuck, and is a commonly used tool to help people who are feeling depressed or fatigued.[7–10]

## Avoiding Avoidance

We've discussed passive coping, which includes avoiding or withdrawing when under stress. While passive coping might give temporary relief, it's a way of coping that can turn into a spiral pretty quickly. The more avoidance and withdrawal go on, the easier it is to be trapped in a negative cycle. Tyler is noticing that over time, it's getting harder for him to leave the house. Sometimes, he doesn't even want to leave his room. The more he avoids, the more he has to hype himself up to do even the simplest of things, making his world smaller and smaller. A key part of behavioral activation will be for Tyler to push himself to tackle things he has been avoiding, even if it feels uncomfortable or difficult.

## Activity Monitoring

Activity monitoring is the first step of behavioral activation. Knowing what exactly you're doing throughout the day, and how it makes you feel, helps you have a clearer picture of what you might need. With activity monitoring, you break down your day hour by hour and rate how your mood during each activity. This can be any system you want. You can use numbers, like a "0" meaning your mood is low during that activity, and a "10" means you feel great. You can also just use a short-hand – A smiley face for activities that make you feel good, a frowny face for activities that make you feel worse, and a neutral face for anything in between.

Tyler was a little freaked out when he wrote down what he did every hour of the day using an hourly calendar and realized he was spending 18 hours a day in bed. Most of that time was sleeping or on social media, which earned a lot of zeros on the mood scale. He wasn't doing anything at all that lifted his mood, and he realized he had completely stopped doing any of the activities that he did before cancer.

## SMART Goals

After looking at an hourly calendar, Tyler knew he wanted to start doing more, but he wasn't sure where to get started. With behavioral activation, it's important to start small and build up activity over time. *Especially* during or after cancer treatment, when you're trying to balance rest and activity and it might be easy to over-do it. It's also important not to set yourself up to fail – if you do too much too soon and get overwhelmed, it's easy to feel discouraged and just get stuck in the cycle all over again.

SMART goals are a way to help set up a measured approach to changing behavior. As outlined in Table 8.1, SMART goals are:

**Table 8.1** SMART goals.

| | |
|---|---|
| *Specific* | What actions will you take? When will you take them? What or who is involved in the action? |
| *Measurable* | How will you measure change? |
| *Adaptive* | A good goal is one that takes you forward in a positive direction. Will this goal help improve your quality of life? |
| *Realistic* | The goal should be realistic. Consider your health, energy levels, time, and whether or not you have the skills to meet your goal. |
| *Time-bound* | How will you know when you've met your goal? When does the goal "end"? |

After doing the activity monitoring sheet, Tyler decided he wanted to spend less time in bed. Using the SMART goal format, as outlined in Table 8.2, this is how he outlined that goal:

**Table 8.2** Tyler's SMART goals.

| | |
|---|---|
| *Specific* | I want to spend a maximum of 12 hours a day in bed, including sleeping. I'll start that goal in two days, after talking to my family about it. I'll set an alarm to get out of bed each day, and I'll ask my parents to help me if I'm having a hard time. I'll plan activities throughout the day in the Activity Scheduling worksheet to motivate me to stay out of bed. |
| *Measurable* | I'll be able to measure change by tracking how many hours I'm spending in bed each day so I can see if I'm making progress over time. |
| *Adaptive* | It is an adaptive goal, because I know that spending all my time in bed is just making me feel worse. |
| *Realistic* | I think this is a realistic goal. I am tired a lot, but I also know that spending time in bed isn't making me less tired. I can always adjust the goal if I need to. |
| *Time-bound* | I'll know I've met my goal if I meet 10 days in a row where I've spent no more than 12 hours a day in bed. I can readjust the goal then with fewer hours in bed if I need to. |

## Activity Scheduling

Scheduling activities can put structure to the day when it feels hard to get a routine started. It can also be a way to make sure you're doing activities that you enjoy **and** that help you feel accomplished. Remember that cycle – the fewer good things you do, the worse you feel. The best way to break out of that cycle is to balance activities that are just for the sake of feeling good *and* ones that help you feel like you're achieving something.

Tyler decides that each day he'll spend some time with his family, reach out to a friend, and start practicing guitar again. He also wants to start to feel like he's doing more to move back toward feeling independent, so he'll spend some time doing research on what he needs to do to go back to college. He knows it will take some time for him to start feeling more like himself, but he feels relieved that he's started to take steps toward feeling better.

**Practice Box 8.1 SMART goals practice**

Is there an area of your life where you need to "press on the gas?" Practice setting a SMART goal here that can help you work toward that goal.

Goal: ______________________________

Specific:

Measurable:

Adaptive:

Realistic:

Time-bound:

*(Continued)*

| **Practice Box 8.1 (Continued)** |
| --- |
| What can you do in the next **24 hours** to start working toward that goal?<br><br><br>What about in the next week?<br><br><br>The next few weeks?<br><br><br>Where do you want to be with this goal in 6 months? |

# 9

# Keeping Track

"*Could I be getting Alzheimer's?*" This is a common question I hear from the people I work with. Feeling less mentally quick or sharp, or feeling "foggy brained" is a pretty common experience after being diagnosed with cancer. You may have heard the term "chemo brain" or "chemo fog" – it's the phrase used to describe this mental fogginess that can happen after cancer treatment. It covers a whole variety of problems related to thinking and memory that usually includes problems with attention and short-term memory, multitasking, organization, confusion, and sometimes finding words.[1] Many people with cancer report symptoms of "chemo brain," with some research suggesting that up to two-thirds suffer with it. Even though this is called "chemo brain," these symptoms have also been linked with hormone therapies, immunotherapy, radiation therapy, and surgery.[1–3] Trouble with thinking and memory can also happen if you have cancer in your brain – whether from a primary tumor, or from cancer from another area moving to your brain. Whether or not this will affect how you think depends on where the cancer is. While this isn't the same thing as chemo brain, you might experience a lot of the same challenges.

There isn't any one cause for chemo brain. Researchers think it's probably the combination of a lot of different things, including loss in white and gray matter in the brain, changes in areas of brain activation, and inflammation that are caused by cancer treatments or the disease itself.[1,4] Some cancer treatments can cause treatable medical conditions that can worsen chemo brain like nutritional deficiencies and anemia. The number and dosage of the treatments you have had, and other factors unique to you like your age, genetics, and other health history can all make a difference in whether you experience chemo brain, how bad it gets, and how long it takes you to recover.[1,4] Even anxiety, depression, or insomnia that isn't treated well can make chemo brain worse.[5]

Chemo brain can be infuriating and can trigger tough emotions like anxiety and isolation. What can make it even more challenging is that it is one of a whole list of "invisible symptoms" that can also happen during cancer, like fatigue and pain. Invisible symptoms are symptoms that other people can't see, unlike hair loss or surgery scars. Because they can't be seen, they seem to be hard for other people to understand. From the outside, you may look like you're managing well, but on the inside, you're very aware of the changes that have happened in how your brain is functioning. Historically, even researchers and oncologists dismissed chemo brain for a long time. No one had a good explanation at the time for why people would report these symptoms, because medical professionals thought that most chemotherapies couldn't cross the blood–brain barrier – the barrier that is the "gatekeeper" making sure harmful substances can't travel to the brain. People with a history of cancer would often also perform in the normal range on neuropsychological and memory tests. They could go back to work and perform well enough, even if they felt it was a struggle.

Now, there is a much better understanding of the variety of ways that different treatments can affect how you think. More recent research using functional MRI, a type of MRI that can show what parts of the brain are operating during a task, also explains why it may look like someone with a history of cancer is still performing fine on memory tests or in their daily tasks. These studies have shown that other parts of the brain may work harder to make up for the parts of the brain that are still recovering from cancer treatment.[6–8] The brain seems to basically build new circuits to recruit other parts of the brain to help recover from an injury. It may look like you're performing "normally" on the outside, but this explains why it feels like you feel different or slower on the inside – because your brain is actually having to work much harder to perform the same task!

So these cognitive challenges are not just "in your head" – they are very real. While chemo brain does usually get better with time, for some people, these challenges might be ongoing. In either case, there are strategies you can use to help yourself manage more effectively and support your recovery. Some of these strategies may seem simple, but they can have a big impact when you use them consistently.

**Reflection Box 9.1 Treatment impact**

How has treatment impacted how you think? Are there any tasks that are more challenging now than they used to be?

## Managing Your Stress

Since a lot of this book focuses on strategies to help you manage stress, I won't spend too much time here. It does feel worth mentioning, though, since stress is one of the things that makes thinking harder. Going back to earlier mentions of the *fight*, *flight*, and *freeze* system, you'll remember that this is an *emergency response system* that is designed to get you out of danger. Your thinking brain takes a back seat; you have less blood flow to areas that are responsible for remembering and planning, while this emergency response system redirects that blood to muscles in your body and the "survival" areas of the brain.[9] The more stressed you are, the less likely it will be that you will be able to think clearly.

### Give Yourself a Break

Staying stuck on what you can't remember or what you can't do is a surefire way to make remembering harder. If you find yourself getting wound up, frustrated, or embarrassed because you can't think of a word or because you're finding a task difficult, take a break. Even a short break of a couple of minutes can be enough to help you reset, and make it more likely that you will be able to perform better on Round 2.

The strategies outlined in Chapter 7 are some of the quickest ways to help soothe yourself. If you find yourself stressed and agitated, it might be helpful to revisit those strategies. They can help in the moment, and they can also build up a good foundation for catching stress before it gets too overwhelming.

### Monitor Your Inner Voice

We've gone over how your inner voice can really influence how you feel. Be aware of any unhelpful self-talk you might be getting into that could be making it hard to concentrate, or that may just be feeding into anxiety and frustration.

It's normal to have thoughts like, "*I'm afraid I'm going to get fired because I keep making mistakes!*" or "*I looked like an idiot when I couldn't remember my neighbor's name!*" Even though those types of thoughts are normal, they aren't helpful, and can fan the flames of stress and frustration. Try to stay away from "shoulds/shouldn'ts" (*"I should be able to do this!"*) and be aware of that inner critic. Also note if you're going off into "what if" territory: *"What if my trouble with memory means my cancer spread to my brain?"* Go back to Chapters 3 and 6 for ideas for redirecting these different types of unhelpful thoughts.

### Practice Paying Attention

Attention is the foundation for memory, and cancer treatments can affect both. You *can* improve attention and memory through mindfulness practice. Review Chapter 4 for help on how to get started shifting from autopilot into a "here and now" focus.

## Rehearsal

### Verbal Rehearsal

We all perform better with practice. The more we can repeat something, the more likely it is that we'll be able to remember it.

Verbal rehearsal is a commonly used strategy for people who are struggling with their memory. It's simple, and just involves repeating information to yourself.[9] This can be new information, like a name of someone you've just met, or simply trying to remember why you're going into a new room. You repeat the information to yourself either out loud, or silently – "*Phone, wallet keys...phone, wallet, keys...*" You can also use this strategy to talk yourself through something as you're doing it to avoid skipping a step, and to help you remember that you completed the task: "*Okay, I'm opening my pill bottle. I'm taking out one pill. It's white and round. I'm putting the pill in my mouth....*"

Spacing this repetition out can also help with training your brain to remember it. For example, saying someone's name that you want to remember – "Sam" – and then waiting 5 seconds. You then repeat it again, and then wait a longer period of time – say 10 seconds. You continue practicing this until it feels more solid. This strategy helps you move information from your short-term into your long-term memory.

### Rhymes and Songs

I'm willing to bet that you have a whole list of silly rhymes or jingles that you've heard taking up space in your brain. I still remember jingles from my childhood (even though I wish I could delete them and replace them with something more useful!). Through a combination of repetition, emotion, and rhythm,[10] it's easier for us to remember songs and things that rhyme. You can use that strategy by setting something you need to remember to a tune. You can be as silly as you want – in fact, the sillier the rhyme or song is, the more likely you'll remember it.

### Visualizing

Just like with rhymes and songs, sometimes our brains find it a bit easier to attach a piece of information to an image. You may have heard reference to Sherlock Holmes' "mind palace," where he associates information with specific locations in a familiar place, making it easier to remember information by attaching it to something familiar.[11] You don't have to create an entire palace, but you might find it useful to attach an image to whatever it is you are trying to remember. You can make it more likely to recall the information by making the image funny, or by associating it with another sense, like a smell.

## Reducing Distractions

You may have found that it is harder to "tune out" noise or distractions following treatment. Remember, your brain is having to work extra hard to recover, so you'll need to do everything you can to try to help it along, including eliminating any unnecessary information that you don't need to focus on. The overall goal is to eliminate any additional information – whether it's visual, auditory, or another sense – that is competing with your focus.

This may mean choosing a quiet setting to meet a friend instead of a busy restaurant, or making sure that the television is off if you're having a conversation. Our mobile devices are also a huge source of distraction. You might find it easiest to silence notifications and pick intentional times to check messages or emails during the day. Multitasking and shifting from one task to another can be much harder after treatment, so help yourself out by not having to restart your focus over and over again every time your phone grabs your attention. Focus on one thing at a time.

You may need to get creative, and do things you haven't done before, like using noise cancelling headphones, or sitting in front of a blank wall to work instead of facing a window. There is no "should" with these strategies – anything you need to help your brain not have to work quite so hard is totally okay.

## Be Strategic

The rest of these strategies are fairly straightforward, but not necessarily easy to implement. I think of them as generally being strategic in how you're approaching day-to-day to help support yourself the best you can. I'm always surprised whenever I meet someone who tells me they've never needed to use a calendar or a "to do" list. I've needed to use these as long as I can remember – otherwise I would never get anything done! Again, you might find that these suggestions are pretty simple, but the difficult part can be in actually implementing them, especially if you've never needed to use them before.

### Using Your Environment

Your environment can play a big part in how hard your brain needs to work to take care of tasks. Set yourself up to succeed by setting up your environment in a way that supports you.

For example – the important things all need to live in the same place. Your phone, keys, wallet, or purse should all be in one location that stays the same. Every time you need to go looking for an essential item, you're experiencing unnecessary frustration.

For tasks that require multiple steps, make it as visual as possible to make sure you don't skip a step. You know how in cooking shows, every ingredient is in its own little bowl? You can do the same to make sure you don't double up salt, or forget an ingredient. You might also find it useful to write down the steps you need to take before a task, and cross them off as you go so that you know you've completed it.

You can build cues into your environment to help yourself remember, too. Put things in places you can't ignore them: A sticky note on your bathroom mirror, or putting something you need to take with you in front of the door.

## Scheduling and Routine

Having a regular routine can be a foundational strategy for memory. Once you've carried out tasks the same way multiple times, you are relying less on memory and more on habit. Having a routine can make tasks easier to remember, such as always taking your medication right before you brush your teeth. The aim is to *always do it the same way*, every time, so that your brain learns that association over time.

Doing this is easiest when you have a regular schedule. This can include using a diary or planner, or putting your daily schedule in your phone as appointments. A schedule can also be a great way to implement some of the strategies discussed in the book. Making an appointment to practice a relaxation exercise, for example, can make it easier to actually build in the practice rather than waiting until you're already stressed or overwhelmed.

Of course, the biggest trick here is to actually *use* the schedule. Set aside a time every morning and every evening to glance at your schedule to make sure you're not forgetting something. I know there are times when I was absolutely *convinced* that I didn't need to look at my calendar, because I just *knew* what I had going on the next day. I've had a lot of embarrassing moments because I insisted that I was right – until I looked at my calendar. Don't be like me – check your calendar daily!

## Prioritize Rest

You will probably need more breaks during tasks than you have needed in the past. Like we talked about with Kim in Chapter 8, you'll probably "hit a wall" with how long you can focus for any given period of time. Work with that and schedule breaks rather than working until you're beyond your max. You might also find it helpful to alternate tasks that are boring with ones that are more interesting to help keep you engaged.

Similarly, it might be useful to alternate more tiring tasks with ones that are less so.

**Practice Box 9.1 Strategies for practice**

Are there any suggestions in this chapter that you've tried?

**Taking Breaks**

**Helpful Self-talk**

**Mindfulness**

**Rehearsal**

**Reducing Distractions**

**Supportive Environment**

**Scheduling and Routine**

**Prioritizing Rest**

Did they help? How much?

Are there any strategies suggested here that you think might be useful to try? If so, which ones?

Is there anything getting in the way of you trying these strategies? This could be a psychological barrier, like *"I shouldn't have to do these things"*; *"what if they don't work?"* It could also be a practical barrier: "My kids are always interrupting me and it's hard to get back on track." Take some time to problem solve below and see if you can come up with some strategies to navigate these barriers.

# 10

# Navigating Your Needs

Communicating during cancer can feel like a full-time job. There is *so* much information being shared – both practical and emotional. You're getting information from your doctors about your disease, treatment, and what to expect, usually in what feels like a rapid-fire foreign language. You're getting phone calls and messages from friends and family asking for updates and checking in. You're fielding well-intentioned "advice," which can range from the useful to the totally bizarre. All while trying to figure out what you need and how to best take care of yourself. Doing this effectively requires *a lot* of direct, clear communication.

Communication during cancer is a huge topic. There are a lot of possible communication scenarios to manage. I knew I couldn't possibly cover everything that might be important, so I decided to focus this chapter on assertive communication around what you need. Asking for help, setting limits with others, and advocating for yourself are all things that many people struggle with. But it's absolutely essential so that you can conserve your energy for managing yourself, rather than managing others. This chapter will offer strategies for getting your needs met in an effective and respectful way.

## Staying Centered

Let's start with a visual. Imagine an archery target. In the center is a bull's eye, with progressively larger rings around the center. Next, picture that the bull's eye represents YOU, the person closest to dealing

*Navigating Cancer: Research Supported Tools to Help You Cope with the Emotional and Physical Impact of Cancer*, First Edition. Jennifer Kilkus.  Published 2026 by John Wiley & Sons, Inc.
Companion Website: www.wiley.com/go/Kilkus/Navigatingcancer

with cancer. In the next largest circle, the one around the bull's eye, is the person that's next closest to the cancer. That could be your partner, parents, other family, or friends – whoever is most involved in helping you cope with cancer. With each larger ring, you'll put the next closest relationships. Close friends in smaller rings, with coworkers and acquaintances in larger ones. As you get to neighbors or other people you may run into, like the cashier at the grocery store, they get put further and further out from the center.

Now, here's the deal: You – in the center – can say *whatever* you want – to anyone in whatever ring – about your cancer. You can complain and curse and be scared and ask for help as much as you want. The people further out can, too – but *only* to the people in larger rings. Comfort IN, dump OUT (Figure 10.1). In other words – people in the outer rings need to look for support anywhere but from you. They can give advice and complain – to anyone but you.

This is called Ring Theory, and it was developed by psychologist Susan Silk[1] when she was coping with breast cancer. She noticed that people would say the most unhelpful things to her – like her coworker who said, "This isn't just about you." Susan thought – "It's not? My breast cancer is not about me? It's about you?" And Ring Theory was born.

Of course it makes sense that people in your life will have thoughts and feelings about your cancer. And there may be some exceptions – if you have children, it would be natural for them to turn to you for comfort and support. For other close relationships, you may decide that you have the energy and desire to have a little more flexibility with what is

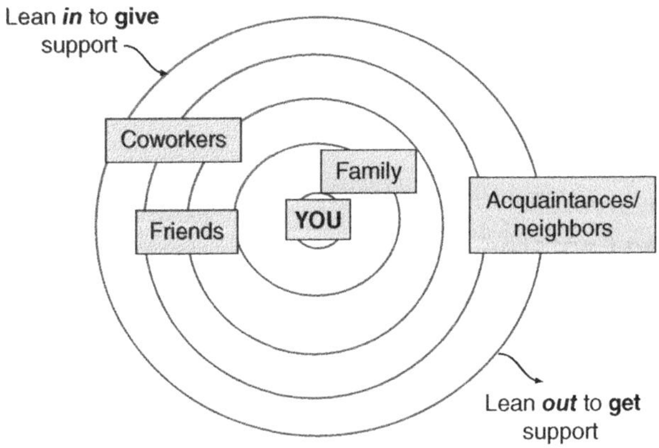


**Figure 10.1** Ring theory.

being shared between the rings. After all, we connect with one another by sharing how we feel. But *please* keep in mind – it is not *your* job to manage the emotions of the people in your life about your cancer. If you're spending energy doing that, you have *a lot* less left over for coping yourself. It also gives you permission to not engage with anyone who has an opinion about your cancer in the outside rings. There's no need for you to use your emotional energy to entertain your neighbor's thoughts or feelings about your cancer treatment. It may be the best use of your energy to stay parked in that center ring.

**Practice Box 10.1 Practice ring theory**

Fill out your own ring below. Remember, you're in the center, with the people closest to you in the next ring.

As the relationships get more distant, the further away they are from the center.

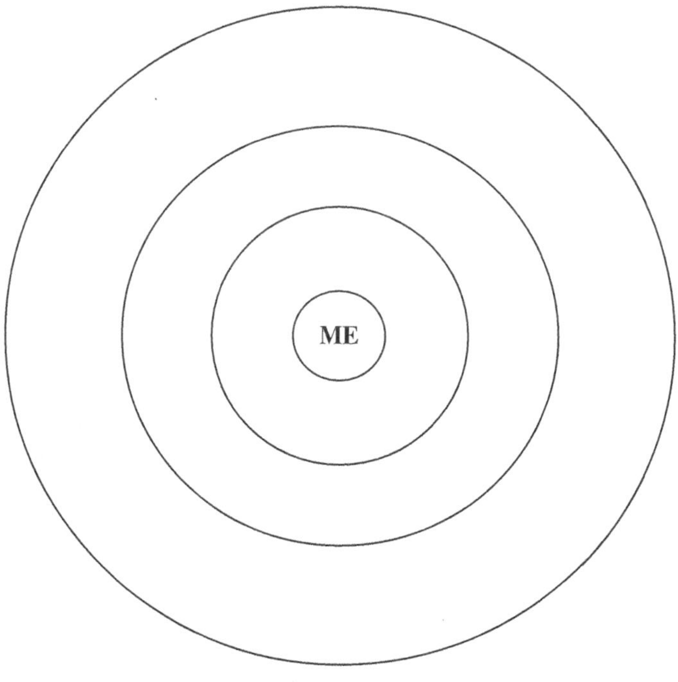

## Asking for What You Need

So now that you're firmly planted in the center ring, I want to help you stay there. Below is a strategy called DEAR MAN borrowed from Dialectical Behavior Therapy (DBT)[2] that focuses on asking for what you need clearly, in a way that is respectful to both you and others. DBT *loves* acronyms, and this skill is no exception – each letter stands for a series of steps that I'll walk you through using the example below, starting with "D."

"D" stands for Describe. The goal here is to clearly and briefly *describe* the facts of the situation without any judgment.

*"You've told your friends about my cancer diagnosis when I asked you not to."*

"E" stands for Express. Try to use "I" statements to express how you feel.

*"I feel frustrated that you keep doing this when I've asked you not to. I want to decide who to share information with, and how much to share with them."*

"A" stands for Assert. Clearly state what you want or need.

*"Please don't tell anyone else about my diagnosis without my permission."*

"R" stands for Reinforce. Explain the positive effects (for the other person) of getting what you want or need. If you need to, here is where you might also outline the negative consequences of not getting what you want or need.

Positive: *"I'll really feel like you're supporting and listening to me if you can do this."*

Negative consequence: *"If you can't do this, I might need to take a break from talking/not share information about my treatment with you."*

"M" stands for Mindful. Being mindful in a conversation means not getting sidetracked, distracted, or pulled off topic. Stay a "broken record." If the other person gets defensive or tries to change the subject, you'll keep making your point.

*"I understand you're upset about our conversation last week, but I want to stay focused on this. Please, don't tell anyone else about my diagnosis without my permission."*

*"You can tell whoever you want if you were diagnosed with cancer. You don't have to agree with my reasons. But please, don't tell anyone else about my diagnosis without my permission."*

"A" stands for Appear confident and effective. Make eye contact, use a confident tone. You don't need to apologize for asking for what you need.

"N" stands for Negotiate. Be willing to compromise if there is space for that in this situation. Focus on what will work and be creative about possible solutions.

*"I know you're having a hard time with this, too. Would it help if I asked my therapist about someone you might be able to talk to for support?"*

Try this strategy the next time you need to communicate something you need. You might think it sounds awkward or uncomfortable. And you're right – it sounds awkward because most of us don't communicate like this. But that's okay; this way of communicating takes practice, and you'll find your own words that feel right with time. You might also be worried that you won't get the response that you're hoping for. That might also be true. A difficult truth about communication is that you can communicate "perfectly," but that doesn't always mean that you get the outcome that you want. Even if you don't, you are practicing prioritizing your well-being, which is always a positive step to take.

**Practice Box 10.2 DEAR MAN**

Think back to a time recently when you were having a hard time asking for what you needed. Try practicing a "re-do" using DEAR MAN.

Describe:

Express:

Assert:

Reinforce:

(Stay) Mindful:

Appear (Confident):

Negotiate:

## Saying No

You've probably heard the phrase, "No is a complete sentence." But we don't usually stop with no, do we? (If we even allow ourselves to say the word at all!). We justify, we defend, we overexplain, we apologize – we might even make up white lies to avoid saying no. If you've made it this far in the book, it's probably pretty clear where I am on the "prioritize yourself" spectrum. You simply won't have the same amount of time, energy, or give a damn that you did before cancer. So that means you have to choose wisely, and that probably means more saying "no." Even if it hurts, disappoints, or frustrates someone else. Saying "yes" when you really want to say no, particularly during a time when you have a lot of competing demands, just leads to frustration and resentment. If you can't set limits on what you give to others now, while facing a challenging and exhausting disease, when can you?

### Challenging Your Beliefs About "No"

Do any of these beliefs sound familiar to you?

*"Saying no will hurt/disappoint other people."*

*"I won't be liked if I say no"; "I am unlovable if I don't give other people what they want."*

*"I need to help other people."*

*"Saying no is selfish."*

Just a reminder that these beliefs aren't facts, even if they feel like they are. They're simply opinions or thoughts that have been shaped over time by experiences and expectations. Challenging these thoughts is the first step to giving yourself permission to say no. That may look like reminding yourself that you always have the right to refuse a request; you're not saying "no" to the person, but "yes" to yourself; you don't *have* to do anything you are asked; you may feel uncomfortable saying no, but both you and the other person making the request will survive you saying no. If you get stuck on challenging these types of thoughts, Chapter 6 has a handful of ideas to come up with more helpful alternative thoughts you can practice to reassure yourself that it is okay to say no.

### How To

If you've not been in the habit of saying no, you might find it tough to know what it looks like. You actually have a lot of options, some of which could feel like they are a better fit than others. The "how" of saying no can also depend on the relationship, with more energy being spent on people closer to you, (in the inner rings) and less on those further away (on the further rings). Below are some ideas to guide you the next time you need to say no.

### Rules of Thumb for "No"

- Be honest and direct: Clear is kind, unclear is unkind. When we waffle because we are afraid of hurting others, we confuse the issue and often end up hurting them anyway.

  Instead of: "*Oh I don't know...maybe.*"; Try: "*I'm not available that day.*"
- Keep it short: Don't overexplain. You really don't have to give all the reasons behind your no – the no is enough. Some people will see explanations as an "in" to argue another point, trying to convince you out of your no. Keeping it short gives people in that category less to argue against.
- Don't over apologize: You are allowed to say no. You are the best judge of your own limits and you are allowed to decide what you do with your time and energy.

### Different Types of "No"[4]

- The Direct "No": Just say no. That's it! Without apologizing. This is a great one for people that you don't have much of a relationship with, like a salesperson or a neighbor.[3]
- The Reflecting "No": This is a validating form of saying no, where you're reflecting and acknowledging the request, but ending with a no. "*I know you're disappointed, but I just don't have the energy to go out tonight.*"
- The Reasoned "No": This no gives a short and genuine reason for the no. "*I can't go tonight, I'm just too fatigued.*"
- The Raincheck "No": This is a delayed no; you're saying no today, but leaving open the possibility that you might say yes in the future. *Don't use this one to wiggle out of something you don't ever intend to do!* This is only a no if you really want to say yes, but just can't right now. "*I really do want to go to dinner soon – I could go next week when I've had more time to recover from treatment.*"
- The Broken Record "No": Incredibly helpful for the times when the other person won't accept your no. You just keep restating your no, without any additional information.

You: "*Oh, I won't be able to. I have other commitments that day.*"

The Other Person: "*But why can't you do it?*"

You: "*I have too much on my plate that day.*"

The Other Person: "*I'm sure you can fit in one more thing, it will only take a few minutes.*"

You: "*No. I can't that day.*"

| **Practice Box 10.3 Saying no** |
| --- |
| Do you have a hard time saying "no"? Are there any beliefs you have about why it's not okay to say no? Write them here. |
| Is there any other way of thinking about this? Is there a different perspective that is more supportive of you? |
| Are there any of the different types of "no" that you have tried? Are there any that you'd think you could try the next time you need to say "no"? |

## Responding to Insensitive Comments

"Foot in mouth" syndrome is absolutely rampant when it comes to cancer. Whether it's fear, thoughtlessness, or lack of empathy, it seems that some people automatically disconnect their brain from their mouth when they hear you have cancer. There are way too many examples to name them all, but I'm sure you've run across them. The people who say, "I wish I could get cancer, maybe I'll lose some weight!"; or tell you a story about their coworker who died from cancer (bonus points if it's the same one you have!); or who give you unsolicited advice, or who tell you they know just how you feel; or tell you that they're tired, too; or who tell you that you should be grateful to be alive, or; ... the list seems endless.

It's hard to know how to respond to these types of comments, because they can take you by surprise. You may also have to judge quickly in the moment based on the type of relationship that you have with the person. You might decide to be a little more generous with a family member than a coworker, for example, and go to the trouble of using a strategy like DEAR MAN.

The below are a few ideas for "one-liners" for responding to these types of comments in the moment when the relationship or the situation doesn't warrant DEAR MAN. It may take some rehearsing, particularly if you are generally a nonconfrontational person. Or if you're like me, and always think of the best comeback about five days too late. But if you're tired of letting these comments go, you might find it useful to choose one or two to keep on hand for when you need them.

- *"That's not helpful."*
- *"I don't want to talk about cancer right now."*
- *"That's an interesting thing to say."*
- *"Why would you say that?"*
- *"I'm not sure I understand. Can you explain what you mean?"*
- *"Do you want to try that again?"*
- *"OUCH."*
- *"That's unkind."*
- *"Wow."*
- [JUST SILENTLY STARE]

**Reflection Box 10.1 Insensitive comments**

Has anyone made insensitive comments to you about your cancer? How did it feel? What did you say? Is there something that you wish you would have said or done in response?

## The Disappearing Act

At the opposite end of the spectrum to dealing with insensitive comments: Navigating the incredibly painful experience of people saying nothing at all. "Cancer ghosting" – the term used to describe when a friend or loved one distances themselves or disappears following a diagnosis[3] – is an all-too-common experience. The reasons that people "ghost" are varied, but they generally come down to fear or ignorance. Fear of you dying, fear of their inability to support you, fear of bothering or offending you, fear for their own health, ignorance of the physical and emotional demands of cancer. Ghosting can also just be plain selfishness or immaturity – people are too uncomfortable or self-interested to show support. Regardless of the reason, it's lonely, confusing, and hurtful.

There is no one right way to deal with cancer ghosting because each relationship is different. You may decide to let go of the relationship, and that is perfectly okay. This person is telling you what you can expect from them, and it's alright to decide that you don't want to make space for that type of relationship in your life.

If you do decide to address it, consider ahead of time what you need from the person who ghosted. Do you need an explanation? An apology? What will you do if a repair attempt is made, and the person disappears again? Think back to DEAR MAN. How can that framework help with communicating what you feel and what you need?

**Reflection Box 10.2 Ghosted**

Has anyone "ghosted" you after cancer? How did it feel?

How did you handle it?

Has anyone showed up for you that you didn't expect?

## Your Rights as a Patient: Communicating with Your Medical Team

Communicating effectively with your medical team can be incredibly challenging. Physicians and other health care personnel are under more time pressure than ever. This time pressure also means that *you* then get put under pressure to try to fit everything important into a really short timeframe. It's not unusual for things to get missed, miscommunicated, or misunderstood. There is also an unspoken hierarchy that exists in medicine. In most places, doctors are still seen as the undisputed "expert" who shouldn't be questioned. That can often make people feel like they can't disagree or ask questions, because they want to be a "good patient." These are real challenges that make communicating about your medical care much more complicated.

I want to be careful when introducing this idea. I don't want to imply *at all* that I think that *you* are responsible for making sure communication with your medical team is effective. One of the most painful parts of my work is to see how often people are harmed by unclear and dismissive communication from their health care team. And I fully believe that the responsibility to improve that lies solely in the hands of the medical professionals. But the reality is that there are a lot of things that "should" happen in the healthcare system that don't. There are urgent changes needed in many aspects of the healthcare system world-wide, like education on effective and compassionate communication and for medical professionals to have more time with patients. These changes will take a long time, and until there is a wide-scale change to address these systematically, you will likely need to be in the driver's seat to get what you need medically. No one will be as invested in your care as you are. Think of this section as less of a "how to," and more of a reminder that you have permission to assert your needs as you navigate your care.

### You Have the Right to Lead Your Appointment

Think of your appointments as a meeting with an agenda. You have a lot to accomplish in a short amount of time, so prepare ahead of time for what you want to address and prioritize what's most important. Outline your highest priorities at the beginning of the visit: *"Good to see you, Dr. Smith. Today I want to make sure we talk about a new pain I'm having in my surgery site, a question I have about my last scan, and to talk about my trouble sleeping."*

Your treatment team often also has an agenda, so there may be some negotiation needed here. But ultimately, your appointment time should be focused on your concerns, so give yourself permission to speak up about what's important to you.

### You Have the Right to Understand Your Disease and Treatment

Not all doctors are great communicators (*this is new information to absolutely no one*). At times, they can rush an explanation, use medical jargon, or may put pressure on you to make quick decisions. If you don't understand something you are being told, or need more time, *please* say so. There is absolutely nothing more important than your health, so *of course* it's okay to ask questions, even if it is either implied or said outright that you are taking up too much time. It is absolutely within your rights to understand what your doctor is saying. This can be as simple as, *"I don't know what that word means, could you explain it to me?"*; or, *"Can you say that another way, I don't understand."*

### You Have the Right to Have Your Concerns Taken Seriously

Sometimes, doctors can dismiss or minimize your concerns. This may not be intentional, but it can still happen. You may need to insist that more information is provided or that a next step is taken. If you don't feel like you're getting an adequate explanation for why a decision is being made, request that your concern is documented in your medical record and that the decision was made not to follow up. If a concern isn't addressed, then it may be time to seek out another opinion, or to change your doctor. Again – it's your health on the line, and trust is a foundational part of a physician–patient relationship. If you don't feel like you can trust your doctor to work in your best interest, or to take your concerns seriously, it's time to find someone else. Someone can be a brilliant physician, but if you feel they are dismissing your concerns, it doesn't really matter how smart they are.

### You Have the Right to Have Support

It can be incredibly helpful to have someone in person with you at your medical visits or at least on present on speaker phone if possible. They may hear something they don't or might ask a question you haven't thought of. They can also give additional information about what they've observed, or even just act as a support for you standing up for yourself if you need to. There may be limits with this – for example, there may be some types of procedures or treatments that a loved one can't be with you for – but there is never a good reason why you can't have a someone with you during a consultation about your care.

## Patient "Bill of Rights"

This is only a handful of your rights as a patient when interacting with your medical team. Most hospitals and medical systems have a "patient bill of rights" that is displayed or can be found online. This can be really useful as a way to understand what the official policy is from where you're receiving your care, so if something isn't going well, you can refer back to it. Please don't hesitate to let someone know if something is happening with your care that you feel like isn't right. People working in the medical profession are humans. They get burnt out, they make errors, and sometimes they're just not nice people. You're not only helping yourself, but you're potentially helping other patients who are experiencing the same problem. But of course, if you take stock and feel like you don't have the energy to make a complaint, that's okay. Conserving your energy and time may be the best way to take care of yourself at that time.

**Reflection Box 10.3 Challenges communicating**

Have you had any challenges communicating with your medical team? What do you think is getting in the way of effective communication?

Have you had to become your own advocate? What has that been like for you?

# 11

# Finding Your Compass: Building a Meaningful Life with and Beyond Cancer

We are all aware of our own mortality. Even though we have this awareness, we don't spend most of our time preoccupied with thinking about it. In fact, some research suggests that our brains actually have protections in place to make sure that we don't get fixated on the idea of dying. A study published in 2019 gives us a clue into one way this works: When faced with the idea of death, our brains automatically categorize that as being information about someone else, not ourselves.[1] That "someday" of death can then feel far off in the future for us, because our brains put it in the category of happening to "other people."

That's until something happens in life that can bring the idea of death more front and center – like a cancer diagnosis. And now, the idea of death is no longer something that happens to other people, or something that will only happen to you someday far off in the future. It becomes much more real and immediate. This comes with a huge challenge: How do you deal with the knowledge of death hanging over you, while trying to focus on living in the only time you actually are guaranteed – here and now?

Anxiety about death is one of the inescapable parts of being human. Whether that anxiety is about dying painfully, leaving those you love behind, regrets about the life you've lived, or what will be after death – it's scary, and messy, and unavoidable. There is no neat, packaged way to take away these fears – I really wish there was. But there are some things that may help you manage these fears and continue to find purpose in the time you do have – however long that might be. This chapter focuses on ways to manage fears about recurrence and progression so that less mental space is taken up by cancer, and how to shift your attention toward building a meaningful life.

## Wrestling with Fear

Fear of having cancer come back, or of it spreading (what researchers call "fear of recurrence or progression") is extremely common. At least 50% of people diagnosed with cancer have a moderate amount of fear (meaning, it's an amount of fear that's interfering with your life), and then about 20% have fear that's severe and disabling to them.[2] That's *a lot* of people who are really struggling with managing this huge amount of uncertainty.

Our minds have a way of filling in uncertainty with predictions and action to try to reduce fear, even if those predictions and actions aren't particularly helpful in the long run. Coping effectively with fear about cancer recurrence or progression relies on a lot of the skills that have already been outlined in this book. Rather than reviewing all of those strategies all over again, I'll focus on helping you identify triggers for fear and then helpful versus less helpful actions to manage it. Then, you'll have the opportunity to put together a coping plan that will include areas to apply skills that have been mentioned in earlier chapters.

### Cancer Triggers

You've probably noticed that after a diagnosis of cancer, it seems like there are reminders of it everywhere. There are *external* triggers, like a television show where a character has cancer, seeing a fundraiser for cancer research, or an upcoming doctor's appointment. There are also *internal* triggers, like having a new ache or pain. In the past, you may have not given another thought to random aches or pains. But now, these physical symptoms equal possible cancer. Whether you've been told there you have no evidence of cancer, or whether you're dealing with an advanced cancer, it can feel like walking through a minefield – no matter how careful you are, an explosion can happen at any moment. Knowing what your triggers are is the first step to being able to develop a plan for coping with fear of recurrence or progression, so let's start there.

| **Reflection Box 11.1 Cancer triggers** |
|---|
| What are your cancer triggers? Record them here.<br><br>Internal triggers: (Pain, fatigue, thoughts, memories)<br><br>External triggers: (Scans, "anniversary" of diagnosis/surgery, etc., scars, stories about other people with cancer)<br><br>What happens to you *physically* when you encounter a trigger?<br><br>What happens to you *emotionally?*<br><br>What goes through your *mind?* |

## Taking Effective Action

Now that you have a bit more information about what triggers worries of cancer recurrence or progression for you, and how you tend to respond, I'll spend some time outlining how to distinguish helpful from unhelpful strategies.

### *Vigilance Versus Hypervigilance*

The tricky thing with worries about cancer recurrence or progression is that it *is* true that you need to pay close attention to your body to make sure that you're taking good care of your health, and so that you can take action to get a symptom addressed if you need to. But there is a difference between *vigilance* and *hypervigilance*. Vigilance would be like taking common sense measures to secure your home. You lock your doors, get renter's or home insurance for emergencies, and may even get a security system. *Hypervigilance*, though, would be if you covered up windows and doors with iron bars, dug a moat, and hired a private security team to monitor your property 24/7. At some point, you might be feeding fear, making it really unclear what is *actually* a threat, versus what just *feels* like one.

Our bodies react to that. Whenever you perceive something as a threat, your body responds, making it even more likely that you'll feel more intense physical symptoms. Then you're more likely to predict a worse-case scenario, and get pulled into a cycle of physical and mental chaos. Checking or scanning your body on repeat is one of the things we know actually makes fear worse, rather than better. Being able to recognize when you're doing this is really important, so you can avoid getting pulled into a cycle that may just make you feel worse.

There is no hard and fast rule to feel safe in your body after cancer. Whether you had symptoms before your diagnosis or not, there may always be a part of you that worries if you're healthy. The aim here is balance – do the common-sense things we know support health, like regular exercise. Make a commitment to yourself to follow up on any symptoms that don't resolve on their own. If you have a gut feeling that something is wrong, keep following up until you get an answer.

### *Getting Good Information*

Sometimes, fear gets worse because we don't have the right kind of information to help manage it. This would be information like knowing what symptoms might be a sign of recurrence or progression, or what the typical side effects for your treatment might be. Getting *good* information is essential, though. You may have had someone on your treatment team tell you not to Google. And they're partially right. Scouring the internet can be a surefire way to continue to feed fear. There's no "bottom" to the internet, so there is no natural stopping point. You can keep searching and searching, and never find what you're really looking for – something that will make you stop worrying. In fact, you're just as likely to find information *to* worry about, keeping the cycle of information seeking going. There also isn't a guarantee that you'll find *good* information on the internet. That doesn't mean that you shouldn't look for information – good information can help alleviate anxiety. But be intentional about what information you're looking for, the source you're finding it from, and identify when you'll give yourself a stopping point for searching. Look for up-to-date information with a recent publishing date, published by an expert in the field, or a governmental or educational institution. Look for facts, instead of opinions, and avoid getting information from social media.

#### *Getting Reassurance*

The difficult thing about reassurance, much like looking for information, is that there probably isn't any one thing that you'll hear that will make you feel better. Instead, you can get into a cycle of continuing to seek out reassurance from others – your doctor, your family or friends – that might temporarily relieve anxiety, but doesn't fully take it away. So then as soon as you start feeling anxious again, you'll go right back to looking for reassurance. It becomes a treadmill that you can't get off of. The goal then would be twofold: To get to a place where you can reassure yourself, and to get to a point where you can accept that there will continue to be uncertainty around cancer, despite what anyone else tells you. This is probably one of the hardest parts of managing these fears and can take time and practice to get comfortable with, so be patient with yourself.

**Practice Box 11.1 Coping plan**

**My Triggers**

Internal triggers: (Pain, fatigue, thoughts, memories)

External triggers: (Scans, 'anniversary' of diagnosis/surgery, etc., scars, stories about other people with cancer)

**My Information Gaps**

What information do I need that I don't have? This could be questions about signs or symptoms of recurrence or progression, or what healthy behaviors you can do to reduce your chance of recurrence.

Who can I contact if I have a concerning symptom?

Who can I contact to get information if I have unanswered questions?

**What about my situation is controllable?** For example, going to all of your appointments or taking your medication as prescribed. If you want to quit smoking, or move your body more, you can set goals for that. Write down anything you can think of that you can control. *(Check out Chapter 8 for help with goals).*

**How can I cope with the uncontrollable?** What can you try to help comfort or soothe yourself when something can't be controlled? *(Chapters 4, 6, and 7 might help here).*

**Is there anything I am doing that may be making me feel worse in the long-run (even if it works for a short time)?** This could be Googling symptoms, calling your doctor every time you have a new pain, or making "what if" or "worst case scenario" predictions.

*(Continued)*

**Practice Box 11.1 (Continued)**

**Is there something more helpful that I might be able to do instead?**
*(Try Chapters* 6 and *7 for ideas).*

## Building Life Around Cancer

The impact of cancer and worry about your future after cancer can feel like it's all consuming. That emotional experience has a lot of similarities with how we tend to think about grief. We generally have an expectation that over time, these difficult feelings will get smaller, and eventually it will feel like there is a way to "move past" it. That one day you'll wake up and you'll be "over" cancer. That might even be something that has been communicated to you by other people – "*But you're done with your treatment. Shouldn't you be over this by now?*" Or, "*You know you're going to have to keep getting treatment. You just have to accept it.*" But grief, like feelings about cancer, doesn't really seem to work that way. So it may be more helpful, and compassionate toward yourself, to think of growing your life around cancer, illustrated in Figure 11.1.[3]

This way of framing coping with cancer and continuing life means that you don't have to force yourself to be in a different place

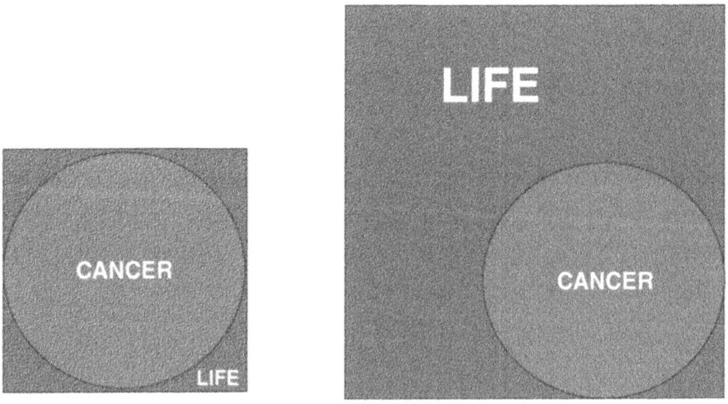


**Figure 11.1** Building life around cancer.

emotionally than you actually are. You also don't have to wait for those painful feelings to go away, or you to feel like you did precancer, before you can start living again. Instead, you can start taking steps now to build a meaningful life. I completely understand that there might be limits to this. I'm sure there are those of you reading who are dealing with treatment for the foreseeable future, or who are really physically limited by your disease. Cancer may continue to take up more space than you want. But is there still a way to make your life *around* cancer as meaningful as possible?

## Finding Your Compass

You might have found that what you view as important in your life has changed after cancer. This is really common – a lot of people feel their priorities have changed after a diagnosis. It can be hard for some people to even listen to the worries of people who haven't gone through cancer, because their perspective of what is worth being concerned about has changed that dramatically.

Any kind of big life event can be an opportunity to reorganize your priorities. As scary as it can be to be reminded that none of us have an infinite amount of time on this planet, it can also give you permission to spend your time on the things that really matter to you. We can think of these priorities, our values, as our compass. They help to orient us – to tell us what direction we want to go with life. Identifying values is an important first step in building a meaningful life around cancer. It also requires you to ask yourself some of the biggest questions in life, that we don't normally ask ourselves: What is important to you? What kind of person do you want to be? What do you want your life to be remembered for? Values help guide you through life and remind you how you want to interact with yourself and the world. One of the great things about values is that there is *no right or wrong*. Your values are what matters to *you*, and it has absolutely nothing to do with what anyone else thinks is important. *You* get to decide.

It can be easy to confuse values with goals. Think of it like this: A value is ongoing, while a goal is something you can cross off a list. A value is, "I want to prioritize my health and well-being," while a goal would be "I'm going to quit smoking" (*Revisit Chapter 8 for more on goal setting*). The value is the overall direction, while the goal is how you get there. That may be why people can often be unhappy once they reach a goal. They expect that achieving the goal – like getting a better job – is the key to being happy. When really, it's the value *behind* the goal that matters. *How* you want to be, instead of *what* you want to achieve. *Why* do you want to get a better job? If the answer is "I don't know" or because "That's what you're supposed to do," you may not be clear on your values. "Working hard and getting recognition for my contributions, and helping to take good care of my family" are values. Getting a better job is a goal that reflects those values. The more we align our life with our values, the happier and more fulfilled we tend to be.

**Practice Box 11.2 The bull's eye exercise[4]**

This exercise is designed to help you identify your values, navigate obstacles, and come up with a plan to start moving toward those values. Take your time with this, and remember, there aren't any right or wrong answers here.

**Identifying Your Values**

Below are four broad life categories – this doesn't cover everything, so feel free to add any that you feel like are missing. You'll answer the question for each area, remembering that you want to reflect how you want to live your life, rather than a specific goal that you're trying to meet.

**Work and education: This area relates to work, career, education, and skills and knowledge development. It also includes volunteering and any other type of work that might be unpaid.**
*What personal qualities do you want to bring to your work? (i.e., focus, dedication, patience). What skills do you want to develop? How do you want to be towards your coworkers, or colleagues?*

**Leisure and Recreation: This refers to how you play and relax.**
*How do you relax? How do you enjoy yourself? What keeps you energized? What kind of hobbies do you have? What do you do to have fun and creativity in your life?*

**Relationships: This category refers to closeness, friendship, and bonding in your life. This includes relationships with anyone important to you: A partner, children, relatives, friends.**
*What sort of relationships do you want to build? How do you want to be in these relationships? What kind of partner, parent, family member, or friend do you want to be? What personal qualities do you want to develop?*

**Health and Personal Growth: This area is specific to your overall well-being and development. This might include religion and spirituality, physical health, self-care, and developing life skills.**
*What are your values related to prioritizing your physical well-being? How do you want to look after your health? Why is this important to you? What religious or spiritual practices are important to you? What life skills do you want to develop?*

**How Fully Are You Living Your Values?** Now that you've identified your values, take a look at the bull's eye below. Make an X in each quarter to represent where you are *today*. An X in the bull's eye means that you are living fully by your values in that life area. An X far from the bull's eye means you are far away from living by your values in that area. Then make a note for each area. For the example below, in Figure 11.2, you might say: *"In the Leisure/Recreation area, I'm in the outer circle. I'm not living my values in this area."* Or *"In the Relationships area, I'm in the bull's eye. I feel like I'm living fully by my values in this area."*

Once you've reviewed the example, try this for yourself in Figure 11.3, and use the next practice box to help yourself identify obstacles and come up with a plan to get closer to the bull's eye with the values that matter most to you.

## Example

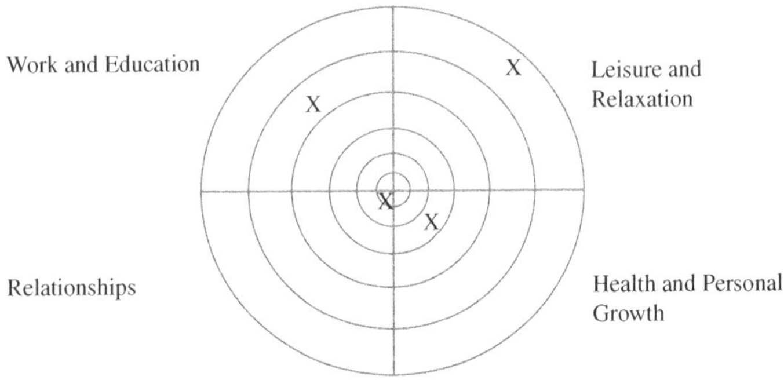


**Figure 11.2** Bull's eye exercise example.

## Practice

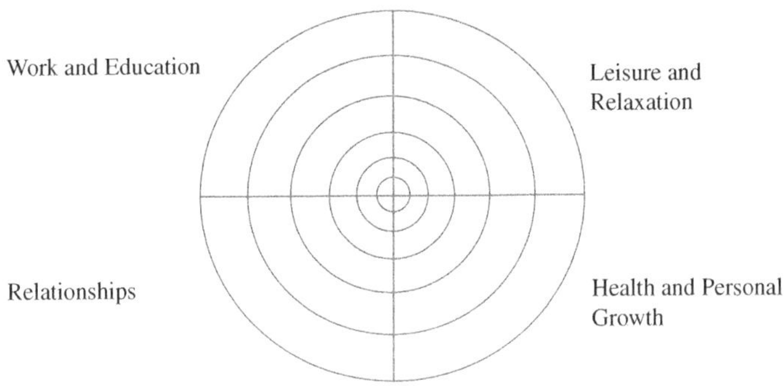


**Figure 11.3** Bull's eye exercise practice.

| **Practice Box 11.3 The bull's eye: What's getting in the way** |
|---|
| **What's Getting in the Way** |

Now, write down what obstacles are keeping you from living your life according to what you value. When you think of the life you want to live and the values you would like to be living by, what's getting in the way? This could be anything from fatigue, to lack of motivation, not being sure where to get started, or conflicting values from other people in your life.

Now, rate how much each obstacle prevents you from living a life in line with your values, on a scale of **1 to 10: "1"** means **"Doesn't prevent me at all,"** and **"10"** means **"It is completely preventing me."**

**Values Plan**

Think about what you would be doing each day that would let you know that you are getting closer to the bull's eye with each of these life areas. This could mean small steps toward a goal, or they could be actions that you were doing that would reflect who you want to be as a person. This may mean navigating around the obstacles you mentioned above by adapting what you do, or by accepting that you may not be able to prioritize this area right now.

Not all of these areas may have the same priority for you – in other words, you don't need to get to the bull's eye in each area if it's not important to you. If that's the case, just make a note about that here, too.

**Work and Education:**

**Leisure and Recreation:**

**Relationships:**

**Health and Personal Growth:**

## Finding Meaning

There have been decades of research on what helps people navigate fears about death. Time and again, the answer seems to point to how effectively people can connect to sources of meaning, even when facing the end of their life. You may have heard of Viktor Frankl, or his book "Man's Search for Meaning." Frankl was a neurologist and psychiatrist who survived the Holocaust and founded a type of psychotherapy that focused on searching for life's meaning.[5,6] He experienced terrible things while captive in four different concentration camps, including the starvation and death of his father, the murder of his mother and brother in gas chambers at Auschwitz, and the death of his wife of typhus. He was known to reference the philosopher Nietzsche who said: "Those who have a 'why' to live, can bear with almost any 'how.'" And despite surviving horrific circumstances, and the death of his family, Frankl truly believed that we never lose the potential to find meaning in our lives, even up until our last moments. He believed that if we feel that life is meaningless, it is not because it has no meaning, but because we have become disconnected from meaning, or have become so demoralized that we can't see the possibility of creating meaning.

Just like with confronting death, we all wrestle with the idea of meaning in our lives, but cancer make it feel much more pressing. Connecting to meaning, regardless of how long you might have to live, can give you strength to cope with even the most desperate of circumstances. What is meaningful is specific to each person, and it doesn't mean you have to find your one true purpose in life, or that you have to be part of some grand plan. Meaning can come in everyday things, like your accomplishments, your relationships, or connecting with life through art or humor. Meaning can also be found in reflecting on how your past limitations or obstacles, which may include your cancer diagnosis, and how you've coped with them.[6]

The rest of this chapter will offer opportunities for reflection on meaning in your life. You might not find any "answers," and that's perfectly okay. These are some incredibly big questions that you may have never considered before. Think back to that idea of growing life around cancer. The idea isn't to get you to a place where you never worry about cancer or death. Instead, the goal is to keep you growing your life around cancer, and to use these questions about meaning to help you find how you can keep doing this in spite of cancer.

**Reflection Box 11.2 Meaningful times**

Think back to times when life felt particularly meaningful to you. It can be something big – like a time when you felt most alive, or something more every day, like a small experience that helped you get through a difficult day.[5]

**Reflection Box 11.3 What am I most proud of?**

What are you most proud of? This could be a role, like being a parent, or an accomplishment, or an activity. What values have these things reflected in your life?

**Reflection Box 11.4 Challenges**

What challenges or obstacles have you navigated in your life?

Viktor Frankl has been quoted as saying, "When we are no longer able to change a situation, we are challenged to change ourselves." What qualities or attitudes have you brought to difficult situations that helped you cope with them?

**Reflection Box 11.5 Connect with meaning**

We can connect with meaning through how we experience love, art, nature, or humor. They can help us feel like we're part of something bigger than ourselves. How have you connected with life in these ways? Maybe you love swimming in the sea, or watching the birds. Or thinking about loved ones, or listening to a beautiful orchestra. Jot down some ways you connect with beauty in a way that feels meaningful to you.

# Part V

# Resources

# 12

# Finding a Team

Navigating your quality of life during cancer can take a whole team. In this section, I've included the different types of professionals that could be useful if you need more support outside this book. Depending on where you live, the names of the professionals or services might be slightly different. There are some professionals that may only provide services in larger cities, but you might still be able to find some helpful information by searching these types of clinics online. Cancer is so challenging – if you need additional support, don't hesitate to ask someone on your treatment team.

## Emotional and Spiritual Well-being

There are a whole host of professionals that can provide support for your emotional well-being. The umbrella term for this type of care is "psycho-oncology," but the term used to describe this service varies from place to place. You might also find it referred to as "support services" or "support programs," "psychological services," "mental health counseling," or "psychological medicine."

Social workers, counselors, and chaplains are some of the most common professionals you can find in a cancer center to help people manage the emotional and practical parts of their cancer care. You might also find nurses or nurse practitioners providing this type of service, too.

*Navigating Cancer: Research Supported Tools to Help You Cope with the Emotional and Physical Impact of Cancer*, First Edition. Jennifer Kilkus.  Published 2026 by John Wiley & Sons, Inc.
Companion Website: www.wiley.com/go/Kilkus/Navigatingcancer

Some locations may also have patient navigators, who help people and their families navigate appointments and referrals.

Psychologists are common in cancer centers, too, but can also be found working in private practice. Most should be familiar with some or all of the strategies I mentioned in this book. You might find it helpful to look for a "health psychologist," to make sure you find someone who has experience working with health challenges. You would look for a "neuropsychologist" or "rehabilitation psychologist" if you're hoping to find someone who can help you diagnose and manage cognitive problems after treatment that aren't getting better with time.

Psychiatrists also play a role in emotional well-being during cancer and are the experts in medications that can help your mood. These types of medications can also sometimes help with side effects from your treatment, like hot flashes, neuropathy, and loss of appetite. Psychiatrists aren't the only doctors that prescribe these types of medications, and can sometimes be hard to find. Your medical oncologist or primary care doctor may also be willing to help you manage your mood with medication. A conversation with them is usually the best first step.

Building a community can also be a fundamental part of your emotional well-being. There is something uniquely powerful about connecting with people who know what it's like to navigate cancer. You may have community cancer support centers around you, or you might find support groups offered where you received your treatment. If you can't find anything nearby, there are also many online cancer support groups and forums to help you connect to others.

## Symptom Management

### Oncology and Palliative Care

Managing symptoms is fundamental for maintaining your quality of life and emotional well-being. If your symptoms aren't well managed, it will be *really* difficult to manage your mood effectively. Your medical oncologist is the "go to" person if you are struggling with symptoms from your disease or treatment. However, if your medical oncologist thinks you might need a specialist, they'll refer you to palliative care or palliative medicine. This is not the same as hospice care. Palliative care is focused on helping you manage your symptoms and improve your quality of life, while hospice care focuses on helping people at the end of their lives. If you don't feel like your symptoms are being managed well, you can always ask your medical oncologist to refer you to palliative care. This type of care may also include pain specialists that would focus specifically on this symptom.

### Hospice

Hospice care includes a range of different professionals that focus on helping people manage all of the challenges that happen at the end of life. Hospice can provide its own service in a hospital or standalone center, but often also provides in-home help, too.

### Physical, Occupational, and Speech Therapy

These professionals focus on helping manage different physical problems that might happen from cancer or from treatment. This could be anything from helping manage lymphedema, pain, swallowing problems, or helping you improve the skills you need to function day-to-day. They may also be able to help you build up your strength before a surgery to make sure you heal quickly, or can help you rebuild your strength if you've gotten weaker from treatment or a long hospital stay.

### Dietician

A dietician is an expert in nutrition, food, and diet. They help with problems with eating and can also help in areas like weight management or how to eat healthier after a cancer diagnosis.

## Specialty Clinics

Specialty clinics have started to become more common in cancer care. This is still a relatively new area, though, and you may not find experts in these areas close to you. It is absolutely worth asking your oncology team, however, if you think you need an expert in these areas.

## Survivorship

A survivorship clinic is a specialized clinic that focuses on supporting you after your treatment has finished. These clinics help with managing the physical and emotional effects of cancer and are meant to help you adjust to life after cancer. These clinics are usually multidisciplinary, which means they may include any of the professionals already listed here, with the goal of focusing on living well postcancer.

## Sexuality/Intimacy and Menopause

Cancer and cancer treatment have a major impact on sexual functioning. Specialty clinics are starting to develop to focus on the specific issues that come up around sexuality and intimacy, including the impact of menopause on women and androgen deprivation therapy on men. Like survivorship clinics, these clinics tend to be multidisciplinary and focus on both the medical and emotional effects of cancer treatment on sexuality. Menopause clinics also address other challenges that come with premature menopause from cancer treatment, like urinary issues and hot flashes.

## Adolescent and Young Adult

AYA clinics are clinics that are focused on the specific needs of teenagers and young adults with cancer. They help with the other issues mentioned in the above clinics, while also helping support people in the age group to get back to school and work. These clinics may emphasize working with the entire family and connecting you to people your age who have also gone through cancer.

## Acknowledgments

Many thanks to you, the reader, for being willing to spend your time with me. I hope that you've found something in these pages that will help you.

I am so grateful for those with lived experience of cancer that took the time to review this book. A very special thanks to Emma Butler, Luke Conroy, Amanda Gillooley, Sara Machnik, Anne Mynes, and Jayne Sheldreck for helping make this book better.

Forever thanks to Dr. Jamie Studts, who first introduced me to psycho-oncology. Thank you for being the supportive and patient mentor that I needed.

Finally, I'm incredibly fortunate to share my life with someone who is unfailingly supportive. Two lucky ducks – thank you for being wonderful, Eric.

# References

## Introduction


1 Machnik, S. (2024). *Crash & Bloom: A Poetry Collection of Grief & Gratitude*. Friesen Press.


## Chapter 1


1 Engel, G. L. (1977). The need for a new medical model: A challenge for biomedicine. *Science*, *196*(4286), 129–136. https://doi.org/10.1126/science.847460.

2 National Cancer Institute. (2022, October). *Stress and cancer*. U.S. Department of Health and Human Services, National Institutes of Health. Retrieved from: https://www.cancer.gov/about- cancer/coping/feelings/stress-fact-sheet.

3 Cancer Research UK. (2025, January 10). *Does stress cause cancer?* Retrieved from: https://www.cancerresearchuk.org/about-cancer/causes-of-cancer/cancer-myths- question/can-stress-cause-cancer.

4 van Tuijl, L. A., Basten, M., Pan, K. Y., Vermeulen, R., Portengen, L., de Graeff, A.,... & Ranchor, A. V. (2023). Depression, anxiety, and the risk of cancer: An individual participant data meta-analysis. *Cancer*, *129*(20), 3287–3299.

5 Lutgendorf, S. K., & Costanzo, E. S. (2003). Psychoneuroimmunology and health psychology: An integrative model. *Brain, Behavior,*

*and Immunity*, *17*(4), 225–232. https://doi.org/10.1016/S0889-1591(03)00033-3.

6 Harvard Health Publishing. (2024). *Understanding the stress response.* Retrieved from: https://www.health.harvard.edu/staying-healthy/understanding-the-stress-response.

7 Queensland Brain Institute. (2019). *The limbic system.* Retrieved from: https://qbi.uq.edu.au/brain/brain-anatomy/limbic-system.

8 Anisman, H., & Merali, Z. (2003). Cytokines, stress and depressive illness: Brain-immune interactions. *Annals of Medicine*, *35*(1), 2–11. https://doi.org/10.1080/07853890310004075.

9 Engert, V., Grant, J. A., & Strauss, B. (2020). Psychosocial factors in disease and treatment—A call for the biopsychosocial model. *JAMA Psychiatry*, *77*(10), 996–997. https://doi.org/10.1001/jamapsychiatry.20200364.

10 Howard-Anderson, J., Ganz, P. A., Bower, J. E., & Stanton, A. L. (2012). Quality of life, fertility concerns, and behavioral health outcomes in younger breast cancer survivors: A systematic review. *Journal of the National Cancer Institute*, *104*(5), 386–405. https://doi.org/10.1093/jnci/djr541.

11 Rosenberg, S. M., & Partridge, A. H. (2013). Premature menopause in young breast cancer: Effects on quality of life and treatment interventions. *Journal of Thoracic Disease*, *5*(Suppl 1), S55–S61.

12 Amidi, A., & Wu, L. M. (2022). Circadian disruption and cancer- and treatment-related symptoms. *Frontiers in Oncology*, *12*, 1009064. https://doi.org/10.3389/fonc.2022.1009064.

## Chapter 2

1 Lazarus, R. S. (1984). *Stress, Appraisal, and Coping* (Vol. 464). Springer.

2 Bandler, R., & Shipley, M. T. (1994). Columnar organization in the midbrain periaqueductal gray: Modules for emotional expression? *Trends in Neurosciences*, *17*(9), 379–389.

3 Obrist, P. A. (2012). *Cardiovascular Psychophysiology: A Perspective.* Springer Science & Business Media.

4 American Psychological Association. (2023). *Passive Coping*. APA Dictionary of Psychology. Retrieved from: https://dictionary.apa.org/passive-coping.

5 Dougall, A. L., Wroble Biglan, M. C., Swanson, J. N., & Baum, A. (2013). Stress, coping, and immune function. In R. J. Nelson, S. J. Y. Mizumori, & I. B. Weiner (Eds.), *Handbook of Psychology: Behavioral Neuroscience* (2nd ed.) (pp. 440–460). John Wiley & Sons Ltd.
6 Löw, A., Lotar Rihtarić, M., & Vrselja, I. (2023). Resource loss, coping strategies and post- traumatic stress disorder symptoms in survivors of the 2020 Croatia earthquake. *BMC Psychology*, *11*(1), 128.
7 Shields, G. S., Spahr, C. M., & Slavich, G. M. (2020). Psychosocial interventions and immune system function: A systematic review and meta-analysis of randomized clinical trials. *JAMA Psychiatry*, *77*(10), 1031–1043.
8 Carver, C. S. (1997). You want to measure coping but your protocol's too long: Consider the brief COPE. *International Journal of Behavioral Medicine*, *4*, 92–100.

## Chapter 3

1 Shahar, G. (2016). Criticism in the self, brain, relationships, and social structure: Implications for psychodynamic psychiatry. *Psychodynamic Psychiatry*, *44*(3), 395–421.
2 Longe, O., Maratos, F. A., Gilbert, P., Evans, G., Volker, F., Rockliff, H., & Rippon, G. (2010). Having a word with yourself: Neural correlates of self-criticism and self-reassurance. *NeuroImage*, *49*(2), 1849–1856.
3 Powers, T. A., Koestner, R., Zuroff, D. C., Milyavskaya, M., & Gorin, A. A. (2011). The effects of self-criticism and self-oriented perfectionism on goal pursuit. *Personality and Social Psychology Bulletin*, *37*(7), 964–975.
4 Neff, K., & Germer, C. (2018). *The Mindful Self-compassion Workbook*. Guilford Publications.

## Chapter 4

1 Nilsson, H., & Kazemi, A. (2016). From Buddhist sati to western mindfulness practice: A contextual analysis. *Journal of Religion & Spirituality in Social Work: Social Thought*, *35*(1–2), 7–23.
2 Young, S. (2016, December). *A pain-processing algorithm*. Retrieved from: https://www.shinzen.org/wp-content/uploads/2016/12/art_painprocessingalg.pdf.

3 Kabat-Zinn, J. (2003). Mindfulness-based interventions in context: Past, present, and future. *Clinical Psychology: Science and Practice, 10*(2), 144–156. https://doi.org/10.1093/clipsy.bpg016.
4 Linehan, M. M. (2015). *DBT® Skills Training Manual* (2nd ed.). The Guilford Press.

## Chapter 5

1 Doka, K. J. (2008). Disenfranchised grief in historical and cultural perspective. In M. S. Stroebe, R. O. Hansson, H. Schut, & W. Stroebe (Eds.), *Handbook of Bereavement Research and Practice: Advances in Theory and Intervention* (pp. 223–240). American Psychological Association. https://doi.org/10.1037/14498-011.
2 Kübler-Ross, E. (1970). *On Death and Dying*. Collier Books/Macmillan Publishing Co.
3 Noack, C. (2024, December 19). At a loss: Facing grief after a cancer diagnosis cancer support community. https://www.cancersupportcommunity.org/blog/facing-loss-grief-after-cancer-diagnosis

## Chapter 6

1 Tomaka, J., Blascovich, J., Kelsey, R. M., & Leitten, C. L. (1993). Subjective, physiological, and behavioral effects of threat and challenge appraisal. *Journal of Personality and Social Psychology, 65*(2), 248–260. https://doi.org/10.1037/0022-3514.65.2.248.
2 Lovallo, W. R. (2005). Central nervous system integrations of the psychological stress response. In *Stress & Health: Biological and Psychological Interactions* (pp. 83–112). SAGE Publications, Inc. https://doi.org/10.4135/9781452233543.n6.
3 Beck, J. S. (2020). *Cognitive Behavior Therapy: Basics and Beyond* (3rd ed.). Guilford Press.
4 Treynor, W., Gonzalez, R., & Nolen-Hoeksema, S. (2003). Rumination reconsidered: A psychometric analysis. *Cognitive Therapy and Research, 27*, 247–259. https://doi.org/10.1023/A:1023910315561.
5 Centre for Clinical Interventions. (2019). Unhelpful thinking styles. In *Back from the Bluez*. Retrieved from: https://www.cci.health.wa.gov.au/~/media/CCI/Consumer- Modules/Back-from-The-Bluez/Back-from-the-Bluez---05---Unhelpful-Thinking- Styles.pdf.

6 Coyne, J. C., & Tennen, H. (2010). Positive psychology in cancer care: Bad science, exaggerated claims, and unproven medicine. *Annals of Behavioral Medicine*, *39*(1), 16–26. https://doi.org/10.1007/s12160-009- 9154-z.

7 Hayes, S. C., Strosahl, K. D., & Wilson, K. G. (2012). *Acceptance and Commitment Therapy: The Process and Practice of Mindful Change* (2nd ed.). Guilford Press.

8 Linehan, M. M. (2014). *DBT Skills Training Manual* (2nd ed.). Guilford Press.


## Chapter 7


1 Munnangi, S., Sundjaja, J. H., Singh, K., Dua, A., & Angus, L. D. (2025). Placebo effect. In: *StatPearls* [Internet]. Treasure Island (FL): StatPearls Publishing [Updated 2023 Nov 13]. Retrieved from: https://www.ncbi.nlm.nih.gov/books/NBK513296/.

2 Dodd, S., Dean, O. M., Vian, J., & Berk, M. (2017). A review of the theoretical and biological understanding of the nocebo and placebo phenomena. *Clinical Therapeutics*, *39*(3), 469–476. https://doi.org/10.1016/j.clinthera.2017.01.010.

3 Benedetti, F., Frisaldi, E., & Shaibani, A. (2022). Thirty years of neuroscientific investigation of placebo and nocebo: The interesting, the good, and the bad. *Annual Review of Pharmacology and Toxicology*, *62*(1), 323–340.

4 Timmers, I., Quaedflieg, C. W. E. M., Hsu, C., Heathcote, L. C., Rovnaghi, C. R., & Simons, L. E. (2019). The interaction between stress and chronic pain through the lens of threat learning. *Neuroscience and Biobehavioral Reviews*, *107*, 641–655. https://doi.org/10.1016/j.neubiorev.2019.10.007.

5 Harvard Health Publishing. (2020). *Understanding the stress response*. Retrieved from: https://www.health.harvard.edu/staying-healthy/understanding-the-stress....

6 Mirzanah, S. A., Yona, S., & Dahlia, D. (2020). Effect of progressive muscle relaxation on sleep quality among patients with chronic diseases: A literature review. *Belitung Nursing Journal*, *6*(2), 30–34.

7 Wang, Y., Yang, L., Lin, G., Huang, B., Sheng, X., Wang, L., ... & Lin, R. (2024). The efficacy of progressive muscle relaxation training on cancer-related fatigue and quality of life in patients with cancer: A

systematic review and meta-analysis of randomized controlled studies. *International Journal of Nursing Studies, 152*, 104694.

**8** Tan, L., Fang, P., Cui, J., Yu, H., & Yu, L. (2022). Effects of progressive muscle relaxation on health-related outcomes in cancer patients: A systematic review and meta-analysis of randomized controlled trials. *Complementary Therapies in Clinical Practice, 49*, 101676.

**9** Hu, M., & Kim, T. H. (2025). Impact of breathing exercises on anxiety and depression in cancer patients: A systematic review and meta-analysis. *Psycho-Oncologie, 19*(2), 3618–3618.

**10** Yau, K. K. Y., & Loke, A. Y. (2021). Effects of diaphragmatic deep breathing exercises on prehypertensive or hypertensive adults: A literature review. *Complementary Therapies in Clinical Practice, 43*, 101315.

**11** Shahriari, M., Dehghan, M., Pahlavanzadeh, S., & Hazini, A. (2017). Effects of progressive muscle relaxation, guided imagery and deep diaphragmatic breathing on quality of life in elderly with breast or prostate cancer. *Journal of Education and Health Promotion, 6*(1), 1.

**12** Kennedy, S. K., Sadeghi, S., Raeisi Dehkordi, S., Lee, S. F., Kirk, D., Cheung, Y. T., & Multinational Association of Supportive Care in Cancer (MASCC) Survivorship Study Group. (2025). Efficacy of multimodal psychological interventions on pain after surgery in breast cancer survivors: A systematic review. *JCO Oncology Practice*, OP2500081.

**13** Correa-Morales, J. E., Mantilla-Manosalva, N., Rodríguez-Cardona, X., Bedoya-Muñoz, L. J., Florez-Vargas, B., León, M. X., ... & Salamanca-Balen, N. (2024). Guided imagery for symptom management of patients with life-limiting illnesses: A systematic review of randomized controlled trials. *Journal of Palliative Medicine, 27*(6), 802–812.

**14** Jacobson, E. (1938). *Progressive Relaxation*. Chicago: University of Chicago Press.

**15** Toussaint, L., Nguyen, Q. A., Roettger, C., Dixon, K., Offenbächer, M., Kohls, N., ... & Sirois, F. (2021). Effectiveness of progressive muscle relaxation, deep breathing, and guided imagery in promoting psychological and physiological states of relaxation. *Evidence-Based Complementary and Alternative Medicine: eCAM, 2021*, 5924040. https://doi.org/10.1155/2021/5924040.

**16** Bernstein, D. A., Carlson, C. R., & Schmidt, J. E. (2007). Progressive relaxation. *Stress Management*, 88 Guilford Publications.

17 Trakhtenberg, E. C. (2008). The effects of guided imagery on the immune system: A critical review. *International Journal of Neuroscience, 118*(6), 839–855.

## Chapter 8

1 Andrews, N.E., Strong, J., & Meredith, P.J. (2012). Activity pacing, avoidance, endurance, and associations with patient functioning in chronic pain: A systematic review and meta- analysis. *Archives of Physical Medicine and Rehabilitation, 93*(11), 2109–2121.

2 Casson, S., Jones, M. D., Cassar, J., Kwai, N., Lloyd, A. R., Barry, B. K., & Sandler, C. X. (2023). The effectiveness of activity pacing interventions for people with chronic fatigue syndrome: A systematic review and meta-analysis. *Disability and Rehabilitation, 45*(23), 3788–3802.

3 Bower, J. E. (2019). The role of neuro-immune interactions in cancer-related fatigue: Biobehavioral risk factors and mechanisms. *Cancer, 125*, 335–364.

4 Al Maqbali, M., Al Sinani, M., Al Naamani, Z., Al Badi, K., & Tanash, M. I. (2021). Prevalence of fatigue in patients with cancer: A systematic review and meta-analysis. *Journal of Pain Symptom Management, 61*(1), 167–189.

5 University Hospitals Bristol and Weston NHS Foundation Trust. (2020). *Managing cancer-related fatigue.* Retrieved from: http://www.uhbristol.nhs.uk/media/3763134/fatigue_presentation.pdf.

6 Mallard, J., Hucteau, E., Schott, R., Trensz, P., Pflumio, C., Kalish-Weindling, M., ... & Pagano, A. F. (2023). Early skeletal muscle deconditioning and reduced exercise capacity during (neo)adjuvant chemotherapy in patients with breast cancer. *Cancer, 129*(2), 215–225. https://doi.org/10.1002/cncr.34533.

7 Mazzucchelli, T., Kane, R., & Rees, C. (2009). Behavioral activation treatments for depression in adults: A meta-analysis and review. *Clinical Psychology: Science and Practice, 16*(4), 383–411.

8 Bower, J. E., Lacchetti, C., Alici, Y., Barton, D. L., Bruner, D., Canin, B. E., ... & Mustian, K. (2024). Management of fatigue in adult survivors of cancer: ASCO–society for integrative oncology guideline update. *Journal of Clinical Oncology, 42*(20), 2456–2487.

9 Fabi, A., Bhargava, R., Fatigoni, S., Guglielmo, M., Horneber, M., Roila, F., ... & ESMO Guidelines Committee. (2020). Cancer-related fatigue: ESMO Clinical Practice Guidelines for diagnosis and treatment. *Annals of Oncology*, *31*(6), 713–723.

10 Sandler, C. X., Goldstein, D., Horsfield, S., Bennett, B. K., Friedlander, M., Bastick, P. A., ... & Lloyd, A. R. (2017). Randomized evaluation of cognitive-behavioral therapy and graded exercise therapy for post-cancer fatigue. *Journal of Pain and Symptom Management*, *54*(1), 74–84.

## Chapter 9

1 Fleming, B., Edison, P., & Kenny, L. (2023). Cognitive impairment after cancer treatment: Mechanisms, clinical characterization, and management. *BMJ*, *380*, e071726.

2 Schagen, S. B., & Wefel, J. S. (2013). Chemotherapy-related changes in cognitive functioning. *European Journal of Cancer Supplements*, *11*, 225–232. https://doi.org/10.1016/j.ejcsup.2013.07.007.

3 Yan, X., Wei, S., & Liu, Q. (2023). Effect of cognitive training on patients with breast cancer reporting cognitive changes: A systematic review and meta-analysis. *BMJ Open*, *13*(1), e058088.

4 Janelsins, M. C., Kesler, S. R., Ahles, T. A., & Morrow, G. R. (2014). Prevalence, mechanisms, and management of cancer-related cognitive impairment. *International Review of Psychiatry*, *26*(1), 102–113.

5 Bai, L., & Yu, E. (2021). A narrative review of risk factors and interventions for cancer-related cognitive impairment. *Annals of Translational Medicine*, *9*(1), 72.

6 Ferguson, R. J., McDonald, B. C., Saykin, A. J., & Ahles, T. A. (2007). Brain structure and function differences in monozygotic twins: Possible effects of breast cancer chemotherapy. *Journal of Clinical Oncology*, *25*(25), 3866–3870.

7 McDonald, B. C., Conroy, S. K., Ahles, T. A., West, J. D., & Saykin, A. J. (2012). Alterations in brain activation during working memory processing associated with breast cancer and treatment: A prospective functional magnetic resonance imaging study. *Journal of Clinical Oncology*, *30*(20), 2500–2508.

8 Apple, A. C., Schroeder, M. P., Ryals, A. J., Wagner, L. I., Cella, D., Shih, P. A., ... & Wang, L. (2018). Hippocampal functional connectivity is related to self-reported cognitive concerns in breast cancer patients undergoing adjuvant therapy. *NeuroImage: Clinical, 20*, 110–118.

9 Ferguson, R., & Gillock, K. (2021). *Memory and Attention Adaptation Training: A Brief Cognitive Behavioral Therapy For Cancer Survivors: Clinician Manual*. Oxford University Press.

10 Jäncke, L. (2008). Music, memory and emotion. *Journal of Biology, 7*(6), 21. https://doi.org/10.1186/jbiol82.

11 Qureshi, A., Rizvi, F., Syed, A., Shahid, A., & Manzoor, H. (2014). The method of loci as a mnemonic device to facilitate learning in endocrinology leads to improvement in student performance as measured by assessments. *Advances in Physiology Education, 38*(2), 140–144. https://doi.org/10.1152/advan.00092.2013.


## Chapter 10


1 Silk, S., & Goldman, B. (2013). How not to say the wrong thing. *Los Angeles Times*. 7 April.

2 Linehan, M. M. (2014). *DBT Skills Training Manual* (2nd ed). Guilford Press.

3 Fitch, M. I. (2025). A new side effect of cancer? *Canadian Oncology Nursing Journal/Revue canadienne de soins infirmiers en oncologie, 35*(4), 532.

4 Powell, T. (2000). *The Mental Health Handbook* (revised edition). Speechmark Publishing, Wesleyan University Press.


## Chapter 11


1 Dor-Ziderman, Y., Lutz, A., & Goldstein, A. (2019). Prediction-based neural mechanisms for shielding the self from existential threat. *NeuroImage, 202*, 116080.

2 Luigjes-Huizer, Y. L., Tauber, N. M., Humphris, G., Kasparian, N. A., Lam, W. W. T., Lebel, S., ... & van der Lee, M. L. (2022). What is the prevalence of fear of cancer recurrence in cancer survivors and patients? A systematic review and individual participant

data meta-analysis. *Psycho-Oncology, 31*(6), 879–892. https://doi.org/10.1002/pon.5921.

3 Tonkin, L. (1996). Growing around grief – another way of looking at grief and recovery. *Bereavement Care, 15*(1), 10.

4 Lundgren, T., Luoma, J. B., Dahl, J., Strosahl, K., & Melin, L. (2012). The Bull's-Eye Values Survey: A psychometric evaluation. *Cognitive and Behavioral Practice, 19*(4), 518–526. https://doi.org/10.1016/j.cbpra.2012.01.004.

5 The Viktor E. Frankl Institute of America. (2024, May 21). *The life of Viktor E. Frankl.* Retrieved from: https://viktorfranklamerica.com/viktor-frankl-bio/.

6 Breitbart, W. S., & Poppito, S. R. (2014). *Meaning-Centered Group Psychotherapy for Patients with Advanced Cancer: A Treatment Manual.* Oxford University Press.

# Index

Note: Page numbers in *italics* and **bold** refers to figures and tables respectively.

Printed and bound by CPI Group (UK) Ltd, Croydon, CR0 4YY

23/08/2026

14947356-0001